Nightmare Pipeline Failures
Fantasy planning, black swans and integrity management

Underground high-pressure gas pipelines pose an immense, but largely unrecognised, threat to the general public. In 2010, two "worst case scenarios" came true when pipelines ruptured in the US states of California and Michigan.

The first pipeline rupture caused a massive explosion and fire, the death of eight people, many injuries and the destruction of 38 homes. The pipeline company was fined $US2.5b.

The second pipeline rupture resulted in the release of vast quantities of oily sludge into a local river system, and many nearby residents having to sell their homes and move. The clean-up cost the pipeline owner $US1b, making it the most expensive pipeline oil spill on land in US history.

Preventing rare events with catastrophic consequences is difficult. In the oil and gas industry (and other industries where organisations operate complex, hazardous technology), incidents arise for a number of reasons, including:

- failure to recognise and act on warning signs
- poor planning and cost-cutting
- inappropriate maintenance
- failure to learn from past incidents and accidents
- poor management decision-making
- inconsistent policies and procedures, and
- lack of effective regulatory oversight.

Analysing and understanding the human and organisational causes of such incidents is, therefore, critical to future incident prevention.

In their latest book, Associate Professor Jan Hayes and Emeritus Professor Andrew Hopkins explore the causes of the California and Michigan pipeline ruptures, providing their insights into how such catastrophic incidents can occur, and how they might be prevented. In addition, they discuss the failure of pipeline regulation in the US and the need for regulatory reform.

DISCLAIMER

CCH

Nightmare Pipeline Failures
Fantasy planning, black swans and integrity management

Jan Hayes
Andrew Hopkins

CCH AUSTRALIA LIMITED
GPO Box 4072, Sydney, NSW 2001

Head Office North Ryde
Phone: (02) 9857 1300 Fax: (02) 9857 1600

Customer Support
Phone: 1 300 300 224 Fax: 1 300 306 224
www.cch.com.au

Book Code: 39745A

ABOUT WOLTERS KLUWER, CCH

Wolters Kluwer, CCH is a leading provider of accurate, authoritative and timely information services for professionals across the globe. We create value by combining information, deep expertise, and technology to provide our customers with solutions that contribute to the quality and effectiveness of their services. Professionals turn to us when they need actionable information to better serve their clients.

With the integrity and accuracy of over 45 years' experience in Australia and New Zealand, and over 175 years internationally, Wolters Kluwer is lifting the standard in software, knowledge, tools and education.

Wolters Kluwer, CCH — *When you have to be right.*

National Library of Australia Cataloguing-in-Publication entry

Creator: Hayes, Jan, author.

Title: Nightmare Pipeline Failures: fantasy planning, black swans and integrity management/Jan Hayes, Andrew Hopkins.

ISBN: 9781925091137 (paperback)

Notes: Includes index

Subjects: Petroleum pipelines—Accidents—United States.
Gas pipelines—Accidents—United States
Pipeline failures—United States
Industrial safety—Management
Industrial safety—Risk assessment.

Other creators/contributors:
Hopkins, Andrew, 1945- (author).

Dewey Number: 363.119665544

Printed in Australia by McPherson's Printing Group

CONTENTS

WOLTERS KLUWER, CCH ACKNOWLEDGMENTS

Wolters Kluwer, CCH wishes to thank the following who contributed to and supported this publication:

Managing Director
Bas Kniphorst

Content Director
Scott Abrahams

Publisher
Javier Dopico

Books Coordinator
Farhana Khan

Project Coordinator
Fiona Harmsworth

Editor
Deborah Powell

Indexer
Graham Clayton, Word Class Indexing & Editing

Cover Designer
Mathias Johansson

Typesetting
Midland Typesetters

ABOUT THE AUTHORS

Jan Hayes
BEng(Hons) (Adelaide), MBus (Swinburne), PhD (ANU)

Jan has 30 years' experience in safety and risk management. Her current activities cover academia, consulting and regulation. She holds an Associate Professor appointment in the Centre for Construction Work Health and Safety Research at RMIT University where she is Program Leader for the social science research activities of the Energy Pipelines Cooperative Research Centre. Jan is a member of the Advisory Board of the National Offshore Petroleum Safety and Environmental Management Authority.

Jan can be contacted at **jan.hayes2@rmit.edu.au.**

Andrew Hopkins
BSc (ANU), MA (ANU), PhD (UConn)

Andrew is Emeritus Professor in the School of Sociology at The Australian National University in Canberra. Over the past 20 years, Andrew has been involved in various major accident inquiries and has undertaken consultancy work for government agencies and large companies. He speaks regularly to audiences around the world about the causes of major accidents.

Andrew has published widely across the field of organisational safety, authoring a number of titles, including the following (published by CCH Australia Limited):

- *Disastrous Decisions: The Human and Organisational Causes of the Gulf of Mexico Blowout*
- *Failure to Learn: the BP Texas City Refinery Disaster*
- *Lessons from Longford: the Esso Gas Plant Explosion*
- *Lessons from Longford: the Trial*
- *Lessons from Gretley: Mindful Leadership and the Law*, and
- *Safety, Culture and Risk.*

Together, these books have sold more than 75,000 copies.

Andrew can be contacted at **andrew.hopkins@anu.edu.au**.

AUTHORS' ACKNOWLEDGMENTS

Some of the research on which this book draws was funded by the Energy Pipelines Cooperative Research Centre, supported through the Australian Government's Cooperative Research Centres Program. The cash and in-kind support from the Australian Pipeline Industry Association Research and Standards Committee is gratefully acknowledged.

We would also like to thank Simon Casey, Barbara Cox, Vanessa McDermott, Richard McDonough, John Muller and Peter Tuft who read the draft manuscript and provided many thoughtful comments.

Thanks, finally, to Deborah Powell for her meticulous and sensitive editing.

CHAPTER 1

INTRODUCTION

The worst nightmares of the oil and gas pipeline industry are coming true in the United States.

High-pressure natural gas pipelines run underground through many suburban areas as part of the network providing fuel to homes and businesses. This infrastructure poses an immense, but insufficiently recognised, threat to the general public. In 2010, one of these pipelines ruptured in San Bruno, a suburb of San Francisco adjacent to the international airport. The result was a massive explosion and fire in which eight people died, many were injured, and 38 homes were destroyed. This possibility haunts many cities around the world.

Coincidentally in the same year, another worst-case scenario came true, near Marshall, in the state of Michigan. A pipeline rupture released vast quantities of oily sludge into a local river system. The smell was so offensive that many nearby residents were forced to sell their homes and get out. The clean-up cost the pipeline owner more than a billion dollars,[1] making it the most expensive oil spill on land[2] in US history.

This book examines the causes of these two events. It argues that, although they were profoundly surprising to the companies concerned, from a broader perspective they were no surprise at all, stemming as they did from well-known human, organisational and regulatory failures.

These two events highlight several ways in which catastrophic pipeline accidents are becoming more likely and the consequences more severe. In part, this is a result of urban encroachment. Gas pipelines are usually built within land corridors designed to keep people and pipelines apart. Over time, however, urban planners encroach on these corridors. The San Bruno pipeline is a case in point. Although it was originally constructed away from housing, the area through which it passed was eventually fully built up, with many residents unaware of the high-pressure gas pipeline in their midst.[3] Over time, therefore, the potential consequences of any pipeline rupture became progressively more catastrophic. As one official report put it,[4] the "decision to allow urban/suburban encroachment along the pipeline right-of-way" was one of the contributing factors to this disaster.

Urban encroachment also increases the *likelihood* of catastrophic explosions, since it increases the likelihood that pipes will be ruptured by unauthorised digging. That was not the initiating event in the San Bruno explosion, but it has been for other high-pressure gas pipeline explosions.

Urban planners would not dream of allowing residential development under high-voltage power lines, but they seem willing to tolerate encroachment on high-pressure gas pipeline corridors. Perhaps the explanation is that high-voltage power lines are imposing and ominous, while underground gas lines are out of sight and readily ignored. Whether or not this is the reason, the willingness of planners to allow encroachment on gas pipeline corridors has increased both the *likelihood* and the *consequences* of high-pressure gas pipeline rupture.

Another factor that is heightening the likelihood of pipeline failure is age. Much of the infrastructure in developed economies is now many decades old, built at a time of lower standards and suffering the effects of time, in particular corrosion. As we shall see, these considerations were highly relevant in the two pipeline failures of interest here.

Finally, the consequences of *oil* pipeline failure are becoming more severe because of the nature of some of the oil that is being transported. Oil is present in vast quantities in the tar sands of Alberta, but it is not easy to extract, nor to transport. After extraction, it has the consistency of peanut butter and can only be transported in pipelines if it is diluted with lighter hydrocarbon liquids. This diluted material is known as "dilbit", short for diluted bitumen. Dilbit is far more problematic from an environmental point of view than conventional oil. The problem is that, while conventional oil floats on water, making it relatively easy to contain in the event of a leak, the bitumen in dilbit sinks, making it much more difficult to remove from waterways.[5] The substance released into a Michigan river system in 2010 was dilbit, and it was probably this fact that made it the most expensive oil spill on land in the US.

The two incidents chosen for study in this book are by no means the most catastrophic events of this type, worldwide. As we write, Taiwan has just experienced its deadliest industrial accident. A pipeline leaked into a stormwater drain running along a busy street and the flammable mixture exploded, killing 30 people and injuring 300 others. The causes are under investigation, but it is known that the pipe was leaking gas in the hours before the explosion.

Another well-known gas pipeline explosion occurred in Belgium in 2004. The pipeline was accidentally damaged by nearby construction work, and when it failed some time later, the leaking gas ignited. The blast was heard several miles away. It melted or burned everything within a 200-metre radius and left a large crater between two factories. Bodies and debris were thrown 100 metres into surrounding fields. Twenty-four people died, most of them emergency service personnel responding to reports of escaping gas, and more than 130 people were injured. The incident highlights the risk to pipelines from third-party activities.

Our impression is that pipeline companies are often more concerned about this risk than they are about the risk of age-related integrity failures, even though, at least in the US, pipeline failures are more commonly caused by integrity issues than by third-party interference.[6] One possible reason for this greater awareness of external threats is that there are obvious and dramatic precursors to externally caused rupture, such as unauthorised digging and, worse, non-penetrating strikes on pipelines. Such events are readily seen as near misses and unmistakable warnings of what might happen. On the other hand, the warnings of integrity-related failure are often more subtle and ambiguous. Be this as it may, both "nightmare" cases that we have identified for study are pipeline integrity failures rather than the result of external interference.

Another disaster that comes into view when we take an international perspective is the oil spillage in Nigeria. This is not a single event but a chronic problem. The amount of oil spilt in the delta of the Niger River in recent years dwarfs all other peacetime[7] spills, including the *Deepwater Horizon* spill in the Gulf of Mexico in 2010. These releases appear to have two main sources: first, the failure of old and rusty pipework (integrity failures), and second, external interference (deliberate interference aimed at stealing oil).[8] The companies claim that theft is the major source of the problem, while environmental groups claim that company failure to maintain the pipelines is the issue. Without entering into this debate, what is undeniable is that the damage to the health and livelihood of local people is immense — far greater than that caused by better-known events such as the *Exxon Valdez* tanker disaster in Alaska and the *Deepwater Horizon* disaster.

If the San Bruno and the Michigan events are not worst in class, the question arises as to why we focus on them here. There are various reasons. First, these two accidents were subject to formal investigation which provides us with comprehensive reports and literally hundreds of primary source documents. This enables us to analyse them in ways that we think are enlightening. For instance, the regulatory failures involved are part of a pattern that has emerged in other major accident events in the US in recent years.[9] By locating these two accidents in this broader context, we hope to contribute to the groundswell for regulatory change in the US.

Another reason for our interest in these two events is that pipeline construction is currently controversial in the US, and the prevention of oil pipeline accidents, in particular, is highly relevant to this debate. We need to distinguish two aspects of the debate. The Keystone XL pipeline (not approved at the time of writing) is designed to bring bitumen from the tar sands of Alberta to the Gulf states for processing. Climate change activists argue that, if all of this oil ends up as carbon dioxide in the atmosphere, it will be disastrous for the planet.[10] The opposition to the Keystone XL pipeline, and others like it, is therefore part of a wider agenda to reduce carbon dioxide emissions globally.

A second argument being mounted against the proliferation of oil pipelines, especially pipelines carrying bitumen, concerns the risk of very damaging releases into the local environment from ruptured pipelines, such as occurred in Michigan. The Keystone XL pipeline, for example, will cross numerous water courses (including drinking water sources), and a good deal of the local opposition to the pipeline is driven by this concern.[11] The risk that water supplies may be contaminated is given credence by the spills that continue to occur from ruptured oil pipelines in the US. Pipeline companies should therefore welcome any analysis such as ours that potentially helps them to reduce the risk of oil spillage, since the fewer the number of major accidental releases, the weaker presumably will be the local opposition to new pipeline projects.

Unfortunately from our point of view, this means that our work can be seen as supporting pipeline company interests in the debate about Canadian tar sands. That is not our intention. Our professional commitment is to help companies reduce the safety risks and local environmental consequences of what they do, not to support them in their quest to develop Canada's tar sands.[12] However, the matter may be largely academic. For one thing, the pipeline company Enbridge has constructed a so-called "clone" of the Keystone XL pipeline (Flannigan South) which is expected to be in business by the time this book is in print.[13] Furthermore, oil is being produced in ever-increasing quantities in the US, and by the time the presidential decision on whether to authorise the Keystone XL pipeline is finally made, the economic rationale for the pipeline may have evaporated.[14]

There is one other unavoidable political dimension to this work. The pipeline companies are locked in battle with rail operators to secure as much as possible of the oil transportation business. One of the factors that influences this contest is the relative safety of these two modes of transport. Rail has not been immune from accidents. One of the most tragic was a train crash in Quebec in 2013. A train carrying light crude oil ignited, killing 47 people. Almost immediately, proponents of the Keystone XL pipeline were arguing that the pipeline should be approved because it was safer than rail.[15] In so far as pipeline companies wish to make use of this argument, it behoves them to put their own house in order and to minimise the risk of catastrophic pipeline accidents. Again, we do not intend to take sides in this matter, but it is clear that our work has the potential to support pipeline companies in their competition with rail for market share.

Two pipeline disasters

We know that some readers may prefer the physical sequence of events that led to each accident to be summarised in one place, so what follows describes the basic facts for the two cases.

San Bruno accident sequence

Just after 6 pm on 9 September 2010, a large fire erupted in the residential area of San Bruno, in northern California. Initial news reports speculated that the fire was the result of a plane crash (since the area is only five miles from San Francisco airport), but it soon became clear that the source of fuel was natural gas escaping from a ruptured high-pressure gas transmission line which runs under the suburb.[16] The pipeline is owned and operated by the Pacific Gas and Electric Company (PG&E). Supply of gas to the fire was isolated after 90 minutes, although the firefighting effort continued for two days. As a result of the fire, eight deaths and numerous injuries occurred, all among local residents. Thirty-eight houses were destroyed and 70 were damaged. The rupture itself created a large crater and a section of pipe weighing well over 1,000 kg was thrown approximately 30 metres.

The section of pipeline that failed is known as line 132, section 180. The failure point was soon identified as a longitudinal seam weld (ie a lengthwise weld turning a sheet of steel into a cylindrical pipeline) that was poorly made when the line was fabricated and installed in 1956. Apparently, no effective integrity testing was done before the line was put into service and it had not been tested or physically inspected in the intervening decades.

Immediately prior to the pipeline rupture, field maintenance work was going on at the upstream Milpitas Terminal. The work interfered with the operation of the terminal inlet pressure control system which led to an increase in gas pressure in line 132. This increase in pressure above normal operating levels apparently caused the faulty weld to fail. Nevertheless, there is no evidence that the pressure in the line rose to be above the designated maximum allowable operating pressure (MAOP). The regulatory requirements for establishing the MAOP by testing were "grandfathered" for old pipelines. Instead, compliance could be achieved by fixing the MAOP at the maximum operational pressure to which the system had been exposed in the previous five years. PG&E had used this method to maintain the MAOP without the need for any integrity testing.

In summary, the pipeline was faulty when installed and had been in service for over 50 years without ever being subjected to any integrity testing or inspection.

Marshall accident sequence

On 25 July 2010, during a routine shutdown, Enbridge's line 6B failed near Marshall, Michigan. The fluid in the line at the time was "dilbit", a *dil*uted form of the *bit*umen extracted from the tar sands of northern Alberta. This was the first major accidental release of dilbit which, unlike other oil, sinks in water and must be recovered from the bottom of rivers and creeks.

The failure of the line was caused by external corrosion. A series of pipeline inspections over several years using devices known as in-line inspection tools or "intelligent pigs" had identified many cracks, including (in 2005) a crack over 4 ft long that ultimately led to the rupture. Despite evidence that this flaw was present, Enbridge had chosen not to excavate this line to further investigate the physical state of the pipeline and conduct appropriate repairs. Instead, its engineering analysis focused on demonstrating that the pipeline did not meet the regulatory trigger for excavation and repair.

The pipeline was operated from a control room in Edmonton, Alberta, and at the time of the failure, operators were shutting down flow as part of a routine procedure. Alarms went off in the Alberta control room but operators did not recognise them for what they were. A relatively small amount of dilbit was released at this stage. Hours later, the operators tried to restart the line. Alarms again went off but the operators did not respond and continued pumping for an hour before they stopped, perplexed that they had not been able to re-establish flow at a point downstream from where, unbeknown to them, the line had ruptured. During this time, a large amount of dilbit was pumped out into a nearby river system. Two hours later, the operators tried again and pumped for half an hour, ignoring alarms. They were considering a third attempt to restart when word came through that a massive release had taken place.

A pipeline with a known integrity problem was not repaired. When it ruptured, the operations people failed to realise what was happening for many hours until they received complaints about the smell of the leaking oil.

Organisational accidents

Social science research has shown that disasters such as these can most usefully be thought of as organisational accidents. Organisational accidents are events that occur within complex modern technologies, such as nuclear power stations, commercial aviation, and oil and gas facilities. They have multiple causes involving many people working in different areas and at different levels. Analysing an incident in this framework involves a search for not only technical causes, but also causes related to systems of work and the actions of people throughout the organisation. Understanding the human and organisational causes is vital for accident prevention.

The most common model of organisational accidents is James Reason's Swiss cheese model shown in Figure 1.1.[17] In this way of thinking about accidents, there is a range of defences in place that are functionally designed to prevent any given hazard from leading to a loss of some kind (such as an accident). In practice, these defences are imperfect (like holes in Swiss cheese). The various hardware and procedural measures in place ensure that failure of any individual measure is not catastrophic.

Hazards

Losses

FIGURE 1.1: Swiss cheese model

An accident occurs when the holes in the cheese line up and provide an accident trajectory through all of the defences.

In this model, the "holes" in the cheese have two interesting features. First, they may be due to active failures, such as the mistakes or non-compliant behaviour of frontline operators, or they may be due to latent failures. Latent failures are weaknesses in the system that do not, of themselves, initiate an accident, but they fail to prevent an accident when an active failure calls them into play on a given day. Problems arise when latent failures in the system accumulate — maintenance is not done, records are not kept, audits are not done. The consequence of a small active failure can then be catastrophic as the protective systems fail to function as expected.

The second feature of the holes in the Swiss cheese is that they are a function of the organisation itself. In this model of accident causation, operator actions in the field are linked to workplace factors, such as competency, rostering, control room design, task design etc, and these issues are linked to organisational factors, such as budgets, safety priorities, management styles etc. In this way of thinking about safety defences, the performance of all components in the system is interlinked.

The concept that accidents occur within an organisational context is key to our social science research and explains why accidents from other industries may have useful lessons for the pipeline industry, even when the technical circumstances of a particular accident may not be particularly relevant to pipelines.

The structure of this book

Interweaving the stories of these two accidents has been a challenge. We wanted to write about the two together because there are so many similarities. But of course there are differences. The difficulty is compounded by the fact that we have more information for the San Bruno gas pipeline explosion than for the Marshall oil release. There were three separate reports on the San Bruno accident,[18] but only one on the Marshall accident.[19] Since we are relying on publically available material, our analysis of the similarities and differences is not as comprehensive as we would have liked.

It is convenient to make a distinction between the way the pipelines were operated and the way their integrity was managed. Our stories diverge most markedly in the way pipeline *operations* contributed to the disasters. Accordingly, Part 1 of this book is an account of these operational matters and treats the two accidents separately. When it comes to managing pipeline *integrity*, the stories are sufficiently similar that we have combined them into a single chapter (Chapter 5). Later chapters also deal with organisational issues that are relevant to both accidents, such as attitudes to safety and remuneration systems. However, they tend to focus on the San Bruno accident because of the limited information we have about Enbridge, the operator of the oil pipeline. The final two chapters deal more generally with issues of regulation and compliance. Because Chapters 5 onwards concern matters potentially relevant to both accidents, we group them together as Part 2. The result is a complex interweaving of both accidents in a way that we believe maximises the potential for learning.

Finally, we have written elsewhere about major accidents in the oil and gas industry, in particular, the 2010 Gulf of Mexico oil spill. We have referred to this accident where we think it useful to draw the parallels.

Chapter summary

The company responsible for the San Bruno pipeline was Pacific Gas and Electric, hereafter PG&E. Chapter 2 deals with PG&E's poor maintenance practices and how these led to the significant over-pressuring of the line that precipitated the rupture. Maintenance often involves the interruption of normal operations and possibly the temporary suspension of normal safety systems. If this is not done with scrupulous care, disaster can ensue. That is what happened at San Bruno.

One of the crucial safeguards against pipeline rupture is the determination of a safe maximum allowable operating pressure (MAOP), coupled with the technology to ensure that this MAOP is not exceeded. Chapter 3 is about how the MAOP was determined. The procedure was not based on any assessment of the risks, but was simply designed to take advantage of what can reasonably be described as a regulatory loophole. The loophole had been inserted into the regulations so that companies operating pipelines brought into service before current regulations were in force could continue to operate their pipelines even though they did not meet current requirements. This is known as "grandfathering". Of course, it is appropriate that human grandfathers be allowed to live out their lives, but whether this is true for safety critical infrastructure is another matter. The San Bruno accident raises acute questions about the appropriateness of this kind of grandfathering.

In Chapter 4, we move to the Marshall accident. When the pipeline ruptured at Marshall, warning signals were received in the pipeline control room thousands of kilometres away in western Canada. But these warnings were ignored, as were the procedures that were supposed to be followed when such warnings were received. As a result, the release of oil and the consequent damage was far greater than it might have been. Chapter 4 explores the reasons the operators behaved as they did. There is in fact a striking similarity between their decision-making processes and those of the frontline staff on the *Deepwater Horizon* whose faulty decisions contributed to the blowout in the Gulf of Mexico in 2010. The chapter is structured around this comparison. It provides a powerful illustration of why it is seldom appropriate to blame frontline operators for their errors and violations.

Pipeline integrity was an issue in both accidents, and Chapter 5 is the first chapter in which we deal with issues that are common to both accidents. For this reason, Part 2 of the book begins here. The way in which PG&E assessed the risk of pipeline failure and prioritised its inspection work was ludicrous. Chapter 5 highlights the many ways in which it made no sense. It is clear that no one ever seriously applied their mind to the rationale of what was going on because PG&E's risk assessment process could never have survived intelligent scrutiny. These are extremely harsh judgments, we know, but we believe the evidence bears us out. We hope that those in positions of responsibility in other companies will feel the need to scrutinise their own integrity management systems with these absurdities in mind. As for Enbridge, its integrity management program was not designed to ensure integrity, but rather to keep the regulator happy. The major failings we have identified provide valuable lessons for all organisations that use risk assessments to manage and prioritise routine activities.

Chapter 6 deals with the meaning of safety. One of the root causes of major accidents in the oil and gas industry in general has been a tendency to focus on personal safety and to ignore process safety. The broader industry is by now well aware of the distinction between these two types of safety and the need to have an independent focus on each type. In the pipeline industry, the distinction between personal and process safety can be reformulated as worker safety versus public safety. PG&E was focused on worker safety to the exclusion of public safety. In so far as our two pipeline companies were concerned about public safety at all, they seemed to believe that all that was required was that they strictly comply with the pipeline safety regulation and all would be well. We demonstrate in this chapter, among others, that this is a fallacy. Finally, we argue that, without a strong organisational commitment to technical expertise, companies tend to adopt a relatively mindless approach to compliance with pipeline regulations.

Chapter 7 deals with two contrasting approaches to rare but catastrophic events. We describe the first as "fantasy planning". Companies often try to convince themselves, regulators and members of the public that they have the relevant hazards under control because they have elaborate plans to deal with them. When it comes to the point, these plans turn out to be wildly optimistic and full of unjustified assumptions and inaccurate data. Their function is symbolic rather than instrumental, that is, they serve as statements that the hazard is under control, rather than as real instruments of control. Fantasy planning was very evident in both accidents.

The second approach adopts the currently fashionable "black swan" metaphor. In Europe, historically, all swans are white, and Europeans could not conceive of a black swan — until they discovered Australia. In the 21st century, the concept of a black swan has taken on new meaning — a rare event with major impact, quite unpredictable at the time, although possibly explicable in hindsight. The 9/11 attack on the Twin Towers in New York was a classic black swan in this sense. Nowadays, major industrial accidents, such as the blowout in the Gulf of Mexico in 2010, are sometimes referred to as black swans. But here the analogy breaks down. Black swans were unforeseeable to Europeans. Major accidents are not unforeseeable to risk analysts. In fact, it is their responsibility to foresee them and to put in place barriers against them. The metaphor is therefore wrong. In fact, it seems to be nothing more than a contemporary version of the idea that major accidents are inevitable. There is a long tradition of this kind of pessimism, another well-known example being the theory of normal accidents, a theory which, on analysis, turns out to be vacuous.[20] Quite apart from this, we find the metaphor irritating because, as Australians, we encounter black swans on a daily basis!

There has been much discussion about fantasy planning and black swans in the wider literature on the causes of major accidents. We have chosen to include these ideas in our subtitle in order to highlight the way our work links to this wider literature.

Chapter 8 discusses senior management priorities. Company bonuses are a clear statement of priorities and those bonuses often prioritise production and profit, rather than safety. That was clearly the case at PG&E, although we have no information about Enbridge. This situation at PG&E was particularly detrimental to safety because, as a regulated public utility, it could not increase profit by increasing charges to customers. The only way profit could be increased was to cut costs, in particular, costs in relation to maintenance and the assurance of technical integrity. This is likely to be an issue for many other regulated public utilities around the world.

Chapter 9 is a discussion of regulatory models. Highly hazardous industries in many countries are required to ensure that the risks are as low as reasonably practicable. This is the criterion against which companies are judged, and from time to time are found wanting. The US pipeline regulatory regime imposes no such requirement. The main requirement is that companies comply with various procedural rules. Whether this results in an acceptably low level of risk is not a consideration. There is in fact no criterion for judging whether the existing risk level is acceptable. The result is that no level of risk is ever unacceptable, provided you have gone through the prescribed process! This remains the case even though a new safety management standard has been promulgated.

Chapter 10 discusses what we call the "compliance paradox". On the one hand, stricter compliance with procedures would have reduced the impact of the Enbridge pipe rupture at Marshall. On the other hand, the compliance mentality with which companies approach regulation in the US is detrimental to safety. Resolving this paradox is vital for safety.

Some chapters have been written so that they can be read in isolation. Inevitably, therefore, there is some overlap between chapters.

Finally, we should say that we have little or no information on changes made since the accidents. One can only hope that Enbridge and PG&E have learnt from their mistakes and are now much more effectively focused on public safety.

Endnotes

1   See http://desmog.ca/2013/08/26/official-price-enbridge-kalamazoo-spill-whopping-1-039-000-000.

2   The Macondo spill in the Gulf of Mexico was many times more costly.

3   Smith, R and Woo, S, "Calls for action emerge after gas explosion", *Wall Street Journal*, 14 September 2010.

4   CPUC, *Report of the independent review panel, San Bruno explosion*, prepared for the CPUC, revised copy, 24 June 2011, p 72. Available at www.cpuc.ca.gov/NR/rdonlyres/85E17CDA-7CE2-4D2D-93BA-B95D25CF98B2/0/cpucfinalreportrevised62411.pdf.

5   Song, L and McGowan, E, "The dilbit disaster: inside the biggest oil spill you've never heard of", *Inside Climate News*, 2012.

6   See http://phmsa.dot.gov/pipeline/library/failure-reports.

7   We take no account here of war-time oil releases such as occurred in Iraq.

8   Amnesty International, *Nigeria: petroleum, pollution and poverty in the Niger Delta*, June 2009.

Amnesty International, *Bad information: oil spill investigations in the Niger Delta*, 2013.

United Nations Environment Programme, *Environmental Assessment of Ogoniland*, 2011.

9   National Commission on the BP Deepwater Horizon Oil Spill and Offshore Drilling, *Deepwater: the Gulf oil disaster and the future of offshore drilling, report to the President*, 2011.

US Chemical Safety and Hazard Investigation Board, *Regulatory report: Chevron Richmond Refinery pipe rupture and fire*, report no. 2012-03-I-CA, May 2014.

10   Avery, S, *The pipeline and the paradigm: Keystone XL, tar sands and the battle to diffuse the carbon bomb*, Ruka Press, Washington DC, 2013.

11   See https://s3.amazonaws.com/s3.350.org/images/kxl-seis-summary-v5.pdf.

12   Not surprisingly, we believe that reducing the amount of carbon in the atmosphere is of paramount importance.

13   See www.huffingtonpost.com/steve-horn/court-key-environmental-l_b_5693271.html.

14   Cushman, J, "What the latest Keystone XL delay really means", *Inside Climate News*, 21 April 2014.

15   Douglass, E, "Does Keystone XL have a place in the oil-by-rail safety debate?", *Inside Climate News*, 17 January 2014.

16   This video shows an early television news bulletin: www.youtube.com/watch?v=EZ6YbUrnxVM&list=LPDs3tGXmbLMQ&index=1&feature=plcp.

17   Reason, J, *Managing the risks of organizational accidents*, Ashgate, Aldershot, 1997.

18   CPUC, *Report of the independent review panel, San Bruno explosion*, prepared for the CPUC, revised copy, 24 June 2011, p 72. Available at www.cpuc.ca.gov/NR/rdonlyres/85E17CDA-7CE2-4D2D-93BA-B95D25CF98B2/0/cpucfinalreportrevised62411.pdf.

CPUC, *Incident investigation report, September 9, 2010 PG&E pipeline rupture in San Bruno, California* (released 12 January 2012), CPUC, Consumer Protection & Safety Division, San Francisco, 2012.

NTSB, Pacific Gas and Electric Company natural gas transmission pipeline rupture and fire, San Bruno, CA, September 9, 2010, pipeline accident report, Washington DC, 2011.

19   NTSB, *Enbridge Incorporated hazardous liquid pipeline rupture and release, Marshall, Michigan, July 25, 2010*, pipeline accident report, Washington DC, 2012.

20   Hopkins, A, "Was Three Mile Island a 'normal accident'?", *Journal of Contingencies and Crisis Management* 2001, 9(2): 65–72.

Part 1

CHAPTER 2

LETHAL MAINTENANCE

This is the first of three chapters on the way that pipeline operations (as opposed to integrity issues) contributed to the accidents. In this chapter, we focus on maintenance work that was being done on the San Bruno line immediately prior to the accident. That work was not properly controlled, leading to an unplanned and uncontrolled increase in operating pressure in the San Bruno pipeline, known as line 132. There is no doubt that this uncontrolled pressure increase caused a faulty weld to finally fail after being in service for over 50 years.

Having said that, it must be acknowledged that the pressure never rose above the specified maximum allowable operating pressure (MAOP) of the pipeline. Given that the formal limit was never exceeded, PG&E argued that the increase in operating pressure was not a significant operational error and hence work practices at its terminal did not contribute to the accident. Based on this line of argument, it is the determination of the MAOP that should be the focus of a study of accident causation, and that is indeed the subject of the next chapter. Nevertheless, it is a fact that, had the pressure increase not occurred that afternoon, the rupture would not have taken place at that time. In that sense, the activities of the maintenance workers were a "but for" cause of the accident, ie but for their activities, the accident would not have happened. This was the view taken by the regulator, the California Public Utilities Commission (CPUC). It said explicitly that problems experienced that afternoon "contributed to Line 132 pipe rupture, even though the recorded pressure at Line 132 did not exceed its established MAOP".[1] Be that as it may, reviewing the sequence of events that led to the higher than normal pressure gives us insight into PG&E's views on risk, procedures and related matters, and it is therefore relevant to our understanding of the organisational causes of serious accidents.

Maintenance work at the terminal

On the day of the accident, field technicians at Milpitas Terminal were making changes to the electrical power system. While the work progressed, gas was still flowing through the terminal to domestic and business users downstream. As the work on the live pipeline system continued, the technicians were in constant telephone communication with operators in the remote control centre. The technicians were trying to understand on the run the impact of their maintenance tasks on the operation of the terminal, and the operators were trying to understand what was happening to the gas network as changes were made at the terminal. Neither group had a complete picture of what was taking place, as will be clear from consideration of the sequence of events immediately prior to the rupture of the line.

PG&E's gas transmission system is controlled from a control room known as the SCADA (supervisory control and data acquisition) centre in San Francisco. The centre operates 24 hours per day, seven days per week. Normal staffing comprises two coordinators and three operators (or two on night shift) working 12-hour shifts. On the afternoon in question, in addition to activity in the control room, three PG&E employees and a contractor were working on the electrical system at Milpitas Terminal, the origin of line 132. Their task was to make some changes to the electrical distribution system at the terminal as part of a bigger, longer-term project to replace the entire uninterruptable power supply (UPS) system. The technicians at the terminal were in telephone contact with the control room operators.[2]

The high-pressure equipment at Milpitas comprises four inlet pipelines and five outlet pipelines, including line 132, plus some associated gas metering and other support facilities. A series of headers and valves links the upstream and downstream sides of the terminal. Each input and output line has a monitor valve which shuts automatically on high pressure, and a regulating valve which is the normal means by which downstream pressure is controlled. On 9 September, only one supply line was open and the supply pressure to the downstream side of the terminal was 361 psig (pounds per square inch gauge, ie above atmospheric pressure).

During the afternoon, in order to install one particular electrical panel, power to some of the control systems was turned off.[3] With the approval of the control room operators, the field technicians changed pressure-regulating valves from automatic control to manual operation to ensure that they would remain open and that gas supply to downstream customers would not be interrupted. At the same time, electronic monitoring of the system was down for about 18 minutes, with the result that the control room operators could not see the valve positions. Once the panel was installed, valves were returned to automatic operation and electronic indication was restored. Other aspects of the maintenance work continued and the technicians noticed that some local indications that needed power to operate seemed not to be functioning. They were unsure as to why this was the case but did not discuss the situation with the control room operators or attempt to fix it. Work continued.

Suddenly, almost one hour before the rupture, the control room operators were faced with over 60 alarms indicating high pressure in various pipelines and reverse flow up some of the supply lines. They spoke by telephone to the technicians at the terminal to try to determine whether the alarms were real and, if so, what the source of the increased pressure might be. During these discussions, the control room operators realised that some of the data they were working with regarding valve positions was incorrect, so no one in the control room could be sure which valves were open and which were closed. They also concluded that at least some of the pressure data was real and the outlet pressure from the terminal was too high, but they did not understand why. The subsequent investigation showed that an electrical system fault as a result of the maintenance work had caused pressure-regulating valves in the terminal to fail to fully open. This exposed the downstream lines to the full pressure of the upstream system. The same fault caused problems with electronic data, too. This resulted in a combination of real high-pressure alarms and spurious valve position data to be sent to the control room — a fault condition that no one expected.

In an attempt to diagnose the problem, a technician manually measured the pressure in the downstream outlet header. He found it to be 396 psig — only marginally below the 400 psig MAOP of the downstream pipelines. Despite this, no attempt was made to shut off the inlet flow to the terminal or to manually close any outlet valves to prevent high-pressure gas from flowing to the downstream pipelines. Rather, troubleshooting focused on adjusting the set points of inlet pressure controllers and outlet monitor valves to try to bring the pressure back under control. Given the difficulties in ascertaining what pressure data was valid and which pressure instrumentation was actually functioning, these efforts were not successful. An automatically operating safety valve (called a monitor valve) on line 132 was set to close at 386 psig to protect that system from overpressure. Due to the time taken for the monitor valve to close, line 132 was exposed to this higher than normal operating pressure for several minutes. Before the monitor valve had completely closed, the operators saw that the pressure in the downstream system started to drop dramatically. This indicated a major rupture somewhere in line 132, although they were unsure of the cause of the low pressure reading at the time.

The leaking gas ignited, immediately resulting in a large fire. Calls to emergency services began within seconds of the rupture and PG&E field staff who happened to be in the area at the time notified the local PG&E dispatch centre. Various PG&E personnel in the area responded and began to coordinate with emergency services. It took over an hour after the rupture for the control room operators to understand, first, that the line had failed and, second, that it was not (as was rumoured in breaking media reports) the result of a plane crash linked to the nearby San Francisco International Airport, nor a gas station fire, but that is was possibly linked to the earlier overpressure event at the upstream terminal.

Clearly, the interaction between the work at the terminal and the ongoing operation of the system from the control room was the immediate trigger of the rupture. The electrical work had significant and unintended consequences. Workers at both locations were taken by surprise and saw their highest priority to keep gas flowing, rather than controlling pressure in the network.

Maintenance procedures in place

Maintenance work with the potential to cause such serious problems when operating high-pressure equipment is normally subject to strict controls. In this case, such control should have been provided by PG&E's work clearance procedures.[4] Systems such as this are commonly used to organise and control maintenance tasks in complex operating systems such as chemical plants, power stations, air traffic control systems, and similar. The primary focus of such a system is to manage the interfaces between the work and the live system by ensuring that all those who might be impacted are aware that the work is to proceed and have given their approval. Other things addressed include points of physical isolation, expected impact on ongoing operations and any contingency planning required.

The work clearance system usually includes a requirement to conduct a basic risk assessment (sometimes called a job hazard analysis or job safety analysis) to ensure that those doing the work are not injured while carrying out the task at hand. This was the case at PG&E and the crew went through this process before the work at the terminal started. Critically, this process included only hazards related to the physical wellbeing of the people doing the work (focusing on fall hazards and the potential for electrocution).[5] No consideration was given to the impact of the work on the gas network itself.

The work clearance documentation contained very few details of the planned work. The forms also included contradictions about the extent to which operations could be impacted, what those impacts might be, and hence what measures should have been put in place, if any, for special operating arrangements (such as operating the regulating valves in manual) during the electrical work. As such, the work clearance system as it functioned was not an effective way to control the maintenance activity and associated risks.

PG&E's work clearance system (and normal practice in this industry) required detailed paperwork to be prepared. The completed forms are intended to describe the work itself and, among other things, its potential to impact operations. The PG&E requirement is that they are to be drafted 10 days before planned work and approved by various people. One single set of forms was completed for all work on the UPS replacement project at Milpitas Terminal covering the period 30 August to 9 September.[6] As such, the operational implications of a large number of specific tasks were intended to be addressed by one blanket approval. The forms note that there is no service interruption expected as a result of the work, but that it will involve an interruption to normal operation of the facility (but no details are recorded, even though this is required). The forms also contain no sequence of the tasks to be performed under this clearance. Such a sequence is required under PG&E's procedures in order to clearly identify when equipment has been cleared for work so that it is safe for the planned task to commence. The same sequence applies in reverse once the work is completed in order to put equipment back into service.

The form was completed by a technician, with the name of the person in charge of the work at the terminal noted as "to be advised". The form was approved by someone from the control room and copies were sent to seven other people across operations, maintenance, engineering and management functions. These copies were labelled as "mandatory" as if receiving a copy has some particular significance. The fact that this paperwork was signed off with such little data included immediately raises the question of what those individuals who signed or received the paperwork were thinking when they gave their formal approval or endorsement for the work to go ahead. Did they think that this work had no potential to impact the gas network? Did they understand that some impact on the operational gas system was possible, but were of the view that it could be safely managed on the run? Were they too busy to read the documents at all or consider the implications? Did they perhaps think that sorting this out was someone else's responsibility?

People in positions of responsibility in hazardous industries routinely give approval for activity to proceed. This may be a formal approval by signing a document or more informal or tacit approval by failing to intervene when notified that work will occur. As the PG&E work clearance procedures say, "Failure to follow these procedures to clear equipment or a pipeline properly could pose a risk to employee and public safety". This means that failure to understand the impact of work on the operating gas system is dangerous and yet the procedures do not explain how to undertake specific tasks. It merely sets out the process by which plans are approved. This approval system failed to prevent the pipeline rupture at San Bruno, so it is relevant to consider in more detail what we are expecting from procedures of this type.

Types of procedures

Work clearance systems, also known as permit to work, are procedures of a kind. It is useful to consider why procedures are so common and what qualities of procedures we are drawing on in expecting them to ensure that tasks are safely completed.

Various authors[7] have proposed that safety rules are of several distinctly different kinds, such as:

- rules that specify goals to be achieved;
- rules that define the process to be followed in order to decide on a course of action; and
- rules that define a specific concrete action or system state.

Goal-based rules give the highest degree of freedom to the decision-maker. This type of rule specifies only the general outcome required and leaves the details of how the goal is to be achieved unspecified.

Process-based rules describe the sequence of steps that the decision-maker is required to complete before coming to a decision about the course of action required. In this case, the detailed outcome is not specified (although a general goal is usually inherent in the context of the prescribed process).

Action rules specify tightly the behaviour required of an individual. They involve much less interpretation than the other types of rules. Examples are hard and fast requirements to wear specific protective clothing to undertake certain activities, or requirements for staff to be licensed in order to carry out certain tasks. Detailed operating procedures are also mainly action rules.

Any real rule may include some features of each of these kinds of rules, but many work management systems (including work clearance systems) are primarily process-based rules. Process-based rules have quite a degree of freedom for those following the rules. The basic assumption behind such systems is that, by involving and informing representatives of different functions, and prompting them to consider a range of specific questions in relation to the planned activity, the interests and perspectives of all functions will be brought to bear on the task at hand and work will be carried out in a safe and timely manner. To put it another way, those following the process as laid down must have sufficient knowledge and experience to bring to the task at hand. Since details are not specified but rather left to the user to determine, this requires thought and judgment. The role of a process-based rule is to focus attention on the most important matters. It is not simply a tick the box exercise.

The clearance paperwork prepared for the UPS replacement at Milpitas Terminal demonstrates that the clearance system at PG&E was not functioning effectively. The procedure is silent about exactly what recipients were to do with the mandatory copies of the paperwork that they were sent, but in this case, the level of detail was so low that they would have found it difficult to make any judgments about the possible impacts of the work based on the information provided.

The significant danger posed by a poor permit to work system is not new information. The North Sea oil production platform Piper Alpha was destroyed by fire in 1988, with the loss of 167 lives.[8] The sequence of events that led to the destruction of the entire structure and all of the process equipment and buildings that it supported began with confusion over permit to work. In this case, under pressure to continue production, operators tried to start a pump that was out of service for maintenance. Because of confusion over the status of the pump due to mishandling of the permit to work paperwork, the operators did not realise that some of the associated pipework was not secure and so starting the pump led to a significant hydrocarbon leak. Of course, there were many other issues with the design and operation of this facility that contributed to the catastrophic result, but it is striking that, 25 years after the events of Piper Alpha, an organisation dealing with high-pressure hydrocarbons had apparently forgotten that permit to work plays such an important role in accident prevention.

Conclusion

The pressure in line 132 rose to close to the MAOP just before it ruptured as a result of maintenance work that led to failures in the pressure control system. The potential for such a problem was not identified by either those directly responsible for the maintenance work, or those responsible for operating the terminal and the pipelines. Safety issues linked to the work were managed on the run, which effectively means they were not managed at all. No contingency arrangements had been put in place and so, when the pressure control system malfunctioned, the control room operators and Milpitas technicians were unable to diagnose the source of the problem before line 132 failed approximately one hour later.

The work at the terminal was subject to PG&E's work clearance procedures. It appears that seven people from operations, maintenance, engineering and management functions were sent copies of the inadequately prepared clearance paperwork. No one chose to intervene. A work clearance system such as this is an example of a process-based rule — a rule that sets down a process to be followed and leaves the content up to those following the rule. Such rules are only effective if all involved understand their responsibility clearly and have the skills, knowledge and professional curiosity to take action to intervene when required. Without such qualities, any process-based rule becomes simply a "tick the box" exercise. An even better option than simply distributing copies of critical paperwork and waiting for someone to intervene is to reverse the onus so that work can only proceed if people sign, so taking responsibility for approval. A work clearance system that functions effectively will ensure that the planned activities have no unintended consequences on the operating system, thus contributing to the safety of all concerned.

It may be tempting to point the finger of blame at the technicians, operators or even those who, by their inaction, approved of the work at the terminal, but these attitudes were apparently so widespread at PG&E that this calls for us to look more deeply at organisational attitudes to disaster prevention. Chapter 6 addresses this issue.

It is perhaps worth noting that, serious as it was, the incident could have been even worse. As the CPUC notes, line 132 was not the only pipeline downstream of the terminal and, "it is possible that one of the [other] pipelines could have experienced pressures far in excess of the MAOP possibly causing other ruptures or leaks".[9] Rather than dealing with the destruction of one suburb, the San Francisco Bay Area could have experienced a series of events of a similar size across the region caused by failures of other lines that also run under or close to residential areas.

Endnotes

1   CPUC, *Incident investigation report, September 9, 2010 PG&E pipeline rupture in San Bruno, California* (released 12 January 2012), CPUC, Consumer Protection & Safety Division, San Francisco, 2012, p 98.

2   Further details of the SCADA centre, the maintenance work being done, and the exact communications sequence can be found in NTSB, *Pacific Gas and Electric Company natural gas transmission pipeline rupture and fire, San Bruno, CA, September 9, 2010*, pipeline accident report, Washington DC, 2011. Available at www.ntsb.gov/doclib/reports/2011/par1101.pdf.

3   It has been suggested to us that work on the UPS, which is a backup system, should have been able to be done without interruption to the normal electrical supply to the operating plant. From the information available, it is not clear as to the overall design philosophy of the power system and the degree of separation between normal and backup power supplies, so we are not able to comment on this.

4   The PG&E work clearance procedures can be found on the NTSB website: NTSB Accident Docket DCA10MP008, Document 260, *NTSB_003-001 S2 WP4100-10 Clearance Procedures*. Available at http://dms.ntsb.gov/pubdms/search/document.cfm?docID=349445&docketID=49 896&mkey=77250.

5   NTSB, *Pacific Gas and Electric Company natural gas transmission pipeline rupture and fire, San Bruno, CA, September 9, 2010*, pipeline accident report, Washington DC, 2011, section 1.9.1.2.

    NTSB Accident Docket DCA10MP008, Document 318, *Interview Transcript of PG&E Technical Crew Leader (Peter Beck)*, p 44ff. Available at http://dms.ntsb.gov/pubdms/search/document.cfm?docID=347730&docketID=49896&mkey=77250.

6   The work clearance form can be found on the NTSB website: NTSB Accident Docket DCA10MP008, Document 54, *Exhibit 2AM: Milpitas Work Clearances, August Thru September 2010 (NTSB_011-008)*. Available at http://dms.ntsb.gov/pubdms/search/document.cfm?docID=343103&docketID=49896&mkey=77250.

7   Hale, AR and Swuste, P, "Safety rules: procedural freedom or action constraint?", *Safety Science* 1998, 29: 163–177.

    Bluff, L and Gunningham, N, "Principle, process, performance or what? New approaches to OHS standards setting", in Bluff, L, Gunningham, N and Johnstone, R (eds), *OHS regulation for a changing world of work*, The Federation Press, Sydney, 2004.

8   Cullen, WD, *The public inquiry into the Piper Alpha disaster*, HMSO, London, 1990.

9   CPUC, *Rebuttal testimony of Raffy Stepanian*, CPUC, Consumer Protection & Safety Division, San Francisco, 20 August 2012, p 36. Available at ftp://ftp.cpuc.ca.gov/SanBrunoReports/CPSD%20Reply%20Testimony.pdf.

CHAPTER 3

MAOP DETERMINATION AND GRANDFATHERING

As described in Chapter 2, the pressure in the failed San Bruno pipeline section just before it ruptured was much higher than normal but still marginally less than the maximum allowable operating pressure (MAOP). Theoretically, the pipeline should not have failed at a pressure less than the specified safe maximum, so this leads to questions about how the MAOP for this pipeline was determined.* A review of the history shows that PG&E engineers determined the MAOP based on compliance with the relevant regulations, rather than by considering the risk involved with operating old facilities under pressure. Of course, the regulatory requirements are themselves based on a generic consideration of risk, and views on what constitutes "safe" can change over time, as we shall see. The pressure-testing requirements for new pipelines which, in turn, fix the MAOP had changed on several occasions since line 132 was installed. This raises the important issue of how to address compliance with current standards for ageing equipment. The way the United States pipeline regulations are structured allows for "grandfathering", that is, for old equipment to receive a blanket exemption from new requirements. This was the case for line 132.

To understand how decisions were made, we must first explain a little of how the strength of an installed pipeline as characterised by its MAOP is determined. In principle, a theoretical value can be calculated based on diameter, wall thickness and material strength. But that is not what happens in practice. The practice is to establish the MAOP by some form of testing to physically demonstrate that the system can withstand internal pressure. Under US regulations, there are two options:

- by hydrotesting** to a pressure well above the proposed MAOP; or
- by deeming that the MAOP is equivalent to the highest operating pressure that the line has seen in the preceding five years.

PG&E had adopted the second method for line 132 because of the cost of conducting a hydrotest for this line and the many others in its system of the same age. As described in Chapter 5, hydrotesting provides the most positive indication

---

* Arguably, if the MAOP had been lower, then more comprehensive over-pressure protection would have been in place for line 132 to prevent high upstream pressures from impacting this line, and so disaster may have been avoided.

** Hydrostatic pressure testing (often shortened to hydrotesting) is a method of checking the strength of a pressure-containing system by completely filling it with water, then pressuring to a fixed value for a fixed time (or via a series of steps) as laid down in specifications.

of the integrity of the system, but it can be expensive and disruptive to gas supply, so it was avoided. The method of deeming that operational history can be used instead of a specific test is sometimes euphemistically called a "service test", ie put the system into service and see if it leaks. This provides no safety margin, as will be discussed in more detail later.

This situation raises several questions:

- How have regulations defining safe operating pressure changed over time and what does this tell us about the safety of existing pipelines?
- What are the safety implications of grandfathering?
- How is grandfathering justified?

These are addressed in turn in what follows.

Meeting regulatory requirements

Californian regulations require that new pipelines are hydrotested to demonstrate their integrity and so fix maximum operating conditions, but requirements for testing old pipelines are "grandfathered", that is, they receive blanket exemption from these requirements. Existing pipelines in the US have been grandfathered since regulations on hydrotesting for new pipelines were introduced in 1961. There have been several major updates to regulations over that time and, despite much debate, the grandfathering exemption for existing pipelines has remained in place (as summarised in Table 3.1).

TABLE 3.1: Regulation of gas pipeline safety in California[1]

Commencement date	Standard/regulation	Requirement (for lines in populated areas)
Pre-1961	No regulation in California. ASME B31.1.8, 1955 typical code.	Hydrotest new lines at 1.1 – 1.4 x MAOP. Not done for pipeline 132.
1961	California General Order 112 introduced based on ASME B31.1.8, 1958.	Hydrotest new lines at 1.5 x MAOP. No requirement for existing lines. No work done on line 132.
1970	Federal 49 CFR 192.505.	Hydrotest new lines at 1.5 x MAOP. Grandfather clause introduced for existing lines, allowing MAOP to be highest actual pressure to which line has been exposed prior to 1 July 1970.
2004	Federal 49 CFR 192.917(e) integrity management rules.	Need to test existing lines like line 132 only if operating pressure is to rise above pressure seen in the last five years.

The first point of interest is that, while there was no specific regulatory requirement at the time, hydrotesting of new pipelines was common practice in 1956 (when line 132 was constructed) and was required by the relevant industry code. PG&E was unable to find any record of a hydrotest being conducted on line 132, and it is likely that the line would have failed such a test due to the faulty seam weld so it seems that the line was not tested when installed.

Regulatory requirements about hydrotesting were first put in place in California in 1961, but they applied to new pipelines only. When the Federal requirements were introduced in 1970, there was significant discussion about what the appropriate safety requirements should be for existing pipelines. The new regulations as initially proposed by the Department of Transportation did not include an exemption for existing pipelines. This would mean that they were required to have a pressure test to confirm that they could withstand pressure 1.5 times their MAOP or, in the absence of any new pressure testing, that their maximum operating pressure should be down-rated from the maximum pressure that the system has ever operated at to allow for the 1.5 safety factor. The Federal Power Commission (forerunner of the Federal Energy Regulatory Commission[2]) made a submission that it had "reviewed the operating record of the interstate pipeline companies and [had] found no evidence that would indicate a material increase in safety would result from requiring wholesale reductions in the pressure of existing pipelines which have been proven capable of withstanding present operating pressure through actual operation". Apparently, as a result of this, the grandfathering arrangements were added to the final version of the regulations, with the result that the safety factor for existing pipelines was effectively set at 1, ie no safety factor at all. As the Department of Transportation noted in the preamble, its agency "does not now have enough information to determine that existing operating pressures are unsafe".[3] In other words, the strategy was to assume safe until there was evidence to the contrary.

We pause to note that this is precisely the wrong approach when dealing with major hazards. In the face of uncertainty, we need to assume dangerous until proved safe. Prior to the ill-fated launch of the *Challenger* space shuttle, a debate occurred about whether certain rubber O-rings would perform as they should, given that the ambient temperature was lower than it had been at any previous launch. Engineers were worried but could not prove that the O-rings would fail. Their managers decided that, in view of the uncertainly and given the fact that the O-rings had never failed to do their job in the past, they would authorise the launch. The result was a disaster that would serve as a lesson to all of the importance of conservative decision-making in such situations.[4]

We will talk further about the problem of using the past to predict the future in this way in Chapter 7. Nevertheless, in 1987, direct evidence of pressure issues in older pipelines surfaced. The National Transportation Safety Board (NTSB) investigated two pipeline failures in which the operating pressures were higher than would be allowed for new pipelines.[5] As part of its response to these accidents, the NTSB made a recommendation that the grandfathering clause be removed and replaced with a sunset clause specifying a date beyond which all existing pipelines would need to comply with the new standard. This recommendation was opposed at the public comment stage and yet again the regulations remained unchanged.

Through this entire period, the determination of the MAOP for line 132 was based on the maximum operating pressure in the last five years as at 1 July 1970, as allowed by the regulations for an existing pipeline. To describe this situation another way, a pipeline that was installed five years before the requirements for pressure testing new lines was in place, operated for a further 49 years without any tests being done. It is instructive to look more closely at the logic behind the concept of grandfathering that allowed this situation to exist and the broader implications.

Grandfathering

Grandfathering of pressure testing requirements has clearly been the source of some conflict between government agencies over a number of decades. Nevertheless, the legislated requirement for line 132 permitted the MAOP to be set by the operating history of the line. This established a MAOP of 400 psig. For a new line with this MAOP, a hydrotest to 600 psig would be required, but for line 132, in service for over 50 years at the time of failure, no such test was required. In fact, 400 psig is higher than the pressure required to supply gas to customers, so it normally operated at a somewhat lower pressure. PG&E's approach was to periodically increase the pressure in the pipeline to 400 psig, simply in order to keep the rating constant.[6] In other words, the pressure was periodically increased for no other reason than to be sure that PG&E could avoid the requirement to hydrotest the line.

In 2004, further changes made to the regulations regarding the technical details behind the grandfathering arrangements gave PG&E an even stronger incentive to ensure that it maintained the maximum operating pressure at an artificially high level. Hydrotesting requirements for line 132 were now directly linked not just to MAOP determination, but also to integrity management. The new rule required that all pipelines needed an assessment (which, in the case of line 132, meant a hydrotest). The rule was designed to require a once-off test of all lines to eliminate the threat of a manufacturing or construction defect. Again, this rule was watered down following public comment so that tests were required unless any possible manufacturing and construction defects could be considered to be stable. The technical argument was made that defects such as cracks that were possibly unstable could grow and lead to failure, whereas stable defects could be seen as not a threat. One of the triggers that required defects to be treated as not stable was "operating pressure increases above the maximum operating pressure experienced during the preceding five years".

The history of the operating pressure of the line was now doubly important as it could be used to avoid the need for hydrotesting that would otherwise be triggered in two different ways. First, operating history was used as the MAOP, rather than having this set by hydrotest. Second, the operating pressure set a threshold that allowed any cracks that might be found to be deemed to be stable, provided the pressure was never increased further, so that again expensive integrity testing was not required. Presumably, the rule-makers failed to realise when setting this criterion that they were giving companies a perverse incentive to regularly increase pressure in the pipeline artificially, even if it were not required for operational reasons, to ensure that neither criterion would be triggered at a later date if operating conditions changed.

Chapter

3

This historical narrative surely shows the danger of a focus on compliance which loses sight of risk. Any assessment of risk would need to consider the threats to the integrity of a 50-year-old pipeline that has never been tested or inspected. Rather, the approach at PG&E before the accident was one focused on compliance with various rules in a way that ensured an expensive test would not be required. As one regulator said during the NTSB inquiry, "artificially raising the pressure in a pipe that has identified integrity seam issues seems to be a wrong-headed approach to safety".[7] He is referring here to what he sees as dubious practices to avoid testing, and to the history of seam weld problems on this line and others. We will come back to the issue of the leak history of line 132 in Chapter 5.

As detailed in Table 3.1, the regulatory requirements in this case are linked to the standards of the American Society of Mechanical Engineers (ASME). Engineering standards are often produced by bodies that are either professional societies or industry lobby groups (or sometimes one organisation that has both roles). This makes the processes of standard writing, especially questions of how stakeholders such as the public and workers are effectively represented, especially important. In its inquiry into the causes of the *Deepwater Horizon* disaster, the Presidential Commission found that the standards of the American Petroleum Institute, which are commonly relied on by companies and regulators in the offshore drilling industry, have essentially been captured by industry financial interests and now represent the lowest common denominator, rather than industry best practice.[8] It is important to note in this case that the grandfathering requirements are in the regulations, not in the standard itself. While we are not specifically suggesting that ASME has fallen into the same trap,[9] in a regulatory regime focused strictly on compliance (rather than risk), referring directly to standards effectively hands the power to regulate an industry on behalf of society to a group of people who are employed by that industry. This clear conflict of interest requires careful checks and balances.

Putting aside for the moment the question of interest groups, standards such as these are sometimes described as "experience carriers". As such, the accumulated experience built into requirements that may be revised over time should be treated with respect, rather than dismissed as irrelevant to old facilities. The fact that no immediate threat linked to existing gas pipelines could be identified in 1970 may constitute a valid reason why a requirement to immediately test or down rate all existing pipelines could be seen as unreasonably onerous. Consider for a moment one alternative approach which would be to insist that all existing pipelines must comply with new prescriptive requirements. Such a blanket requirement would be very costly in some cases, effectively requiring old systems to be replaced due to the cost of upgrade. With no consideration of the actual benefit that would result in any given case, a blanket requirement to comply is as unreasonable as a blanket exemption.

On the other hand, it does not explain why such lines should be allowed to operate indefinitely with no safety margin. A better approach would be based on risk — what is the risk that the revised requirements are designed to address? For facilities that do not comply with the new requirements, is this risk relevant and how else is it mitigated? If changes need to be made, what is a reasonable time frame based on risk exposure? This is how compliance with standards is treated in a duty of care safety regulatory regime, as is discussed further in Chapter 9.

The problem of many hands

In defence of this approach to MAOP determination and the management of defects, PG&E's Manager of Integrity Management gave evidence soon after the accident that "the maximum allowable operating pressure is a pressure with significant safety factors built in already … the pipeline is tested to a much greater pressure when it is manufactured … so raising the pressure up [to a higher than normal operating pressure to keep the grandfathered MAOP] … is not a cause for concern".[10]

Note the logic of that argument. While the testing arrangements after installation for new pipelines have required a 1.5 safety factor since 1961, in this manager's view, existing pipelines were not required to have any safety margin at all above their normal operating pressure because there are other risk controls in place. Specifically, he is claiming credit for the testing of sections of pipe that is typically done when they are manufactured. As we now know, for line 132, it is unlikely that *any* testing took place in 1956 because the section that ultimately ruptured would have failed such a test.[11] Testing to establish a MAOP for the system that includes a safety margin is one barrier aimed at preventing pipeline leaks. In his comment above, the manager is defending much less conservative practices around the setting of the MAOP on the basis that the integrity of this barrier is not important because other barriers are in place and are robust. In this case, he is specifically referring to testing during manufacturing and construction of the pipe itself. As we now know, the manufacturing was faulty and so this barrier too was flawed.

When making this argument, the manager is relying on the concept of defence in depth — that effective risk control requires multiple barriers to be in place. As the well-known metaphor of Swiss cheese described in Chapter 1 reminds us, because risk controls or barriers are never 100% effective, a robust system has many barriers in place to prevent a hazard from leading to an accident. This metaphor is certainly not meant to relieve people of motivation to ensure that the barriers for which they are responsible function effectively, on the basis that accidents will be prevented by the actions of others. Social psychologists call this behaviour "social loafing", based on experiments that demonstrate that people working in a group often put in less effort than when they are working individually.[12] This concept also applies at an organisational level and has been implicated in accident causation previously. In his analysis of the *Blackhawk* friendly fire incident in Iraq, Snook asserts that responsibility was "spread so thin by the laws of social impact and confused authority relationships that no one felt compelled to act. Hence a weak team with diffuse responsibilities contributed to this accident by its silence".[13]

Specifically, a problematic attitude that can develop when a broad group of people work collectively on a complex task can be characterised as "it doesn't matter if my part of the system doesn't work properly because everyone else is doing their job well, even if I'm not". Looking at this issue from outside the group, this is known as the problem of many hands,[14] that is, where responsibility for safety is distributed across a wide group of people and so it is difficult to ascribe responsibility to individuals, either proactively or even retrospectively (ie following an accident).

Engineering systems are particularly vulnerable to safety issues that require people to take action in their everyday work to prevent bad outcomes long into the future. When lives are ultimately at stake, taking responsibility becomes a matter of ethics. Ethics is linked to morality and to questions of blame, and is discussed at length in fields such as medicine and aviation, but much less so in engineering.[14] In these other sectors, professional judgments are made typically by individuals. Cause and effect is typically clear and direct, with consequences playing out in the near term. If a doctor or nurse makes a mistake when treating a patient, the result is usually obvious and immediate. In such cases, responsibility is quite clear.[15] Engineering judgments have different qualities which make individual responsibility more complex. Safety is often a collective responsibility with uncertain impacts felt over an extended time frame, which makes questions of the morality of individual decisions much easier to avoid.

Returning to San Bruno, the best estimate of the pressure at the failure point at the time the rupture occurred is 386 psig, so we know that that the line failed within the pressure envelope allowed by the code and the regulations. CPUC argues that this is because of an unstable manufacturing defect and that the cyclic loading presented on the system by PG&E's regime of MAOP maintenance may have caused a fatigue failure. This is discussed at length in CPUC evidence.[16] Over many years, PG&E chose to focus on the wrong thing. PG&E engineers were using their considerable engineering problem-solving skills to avoid the need for hydrotesting, rather than considering the moral dimension of their work, ie the impact of their actions on the safety of the general public. In the long run, they would have better served their organisation by using their skills to solve a different problem — that of identifying possible failure mechanisms and more conservatively determining the MAOP as a result, even if this led to the decision to test the pipeline, incurring the resultant costs.

These issues are discussed further in Chapter 6.

Conclusion

Line 132 failed at a pressure below its specified maximum allowable operating pressure (MAOP). The MAOP for the line was set based on past operating history, rather than by testing (as has been required for any new pipeline since 1970). This method of setting the MAOP includes no safety margin, but is allowable under regulation due to "grandfathering" which gives blanket exemption for existing facilities from new safety requirements.

The process of grandfathering is an administrative exercise divorced from integrity management considerations as it assumes no construction defects, no subsequent damage and no time-dependent deterioration. It also takes no account of the consequences of failure in a populated area. Grandfathering (this time, of requirements for flaring and venting) was also highlighted as a significant causal factor in the BP Texas City Refinery disaster in 2005 in which 15 people died.[17] Rather than giving a blanket exemption (or requiring blanket compliance) of old facilities to new safety standards, a risk-based approach should be used which puts the burden of proof onto the operators of old facilities to demonstrate that the risk of continuing to operate without compliance to new requirements is insignificant.

PG&E adopted an attitude of compliance with the regulations on MAOP, rather than considering risk and the possible implications of their actions. Individuals appear to have been taken in by the problem of many hands where no one takes responsibility for outcomes when systems are complex and responsibility is widely distributed. When safety is routinely viewed as someone else's responsibility, latent failures will accumulate over time with potentially catastrophic results.

Endnotes

1   Summarised from NTSB, *Pacific Gas and Electric Company natural gas transmission pipeline rupture and fire, San Bruno, CA, September 9, 2010*, pipeline accident report, Washington DC, 2011, section 1.7.5.

2   The Federal Energy Regulatory Commission is the primary regulator for the gas pipeline industry in the US, controlling project approvals and pricing etc, whereas the Department of Transportation's Office of Pipeline Safety is responsible specifically for safety regulation.

3   Quoted in NTSB, *Pacific Gas and Electric Company natural gas transmission pipeline rupture and fire, San Bruno, CA, September 9, 2010*, pipeline accident report, Washington DC, 2011, p 35.

4   For more about the *Challenger* disaster, see Vaughan, D, *The Challenger launch decision: risky technology, culture and deviance at NASA*, University of Chicago Press, Chicago, 1996.

5   See NTSB, *Texas Eastern Gas Pipeline Company ruptures and fires at Beaumont, Kentucky, on April 27, 1985, and Lancaster, Kentucky, on February 21, 1986*, pipeline accident report NTSB/PAR-87/01, Washington DC, 1987.

6   Details can be found in NTSB Accident Docket DCA10MP008, Document 218, *Public Hearing Transcript - March 1, 2011 (Day One)*, p 83, line 8ff. Available at http://dms.ntsb.gov/pubdms/ search/document.cfm?docID=344892&docketID=49896&mkey=77250.

7   NTSB, *Pacific Gas and Electric Company natural gas transmission pipeline rupture and fire, San Bruno, CA, September 9, 2010*, pipeline accident report, Washington DC, 2011, p 37.

8   National Commission on the BP Deepwater Horizon Oil Spill and Offshore Drilling, *Deepwater: the Gulf oil disaster and the future of offshore drilling, report to the President*, 2011, ch 8.

9   The extent to which ASME standards represent industry commercial interests, rather than best practice for safety, was famously questioned by Admiral Rickover several decades ago. We have not investigated this issue and so are not in a position to comment on current practices. See Joint Committee on Atomic Energy, naval nuclear propulsion program, testimony of Vice Admiral HG Rickover, second session, Washington DC, 19 and 20 March 1970.

10   NTSB Accident Docket DCA10MP008, Document 218, *Public Hearing Transcript - March 1, 2011 (Day One)*. Available at http://dms.ntsb.gov/pubdms/search/document.cfm?docID=34489 2&docketID=49896&mkey=77250.

11   The section of line 132 that ruptured was not part of the original pipeline, but rather a section that was relocated in 1956 due to the new housing development in the area. When this work was done, this section of the pipeline was made up of several short pipe sections (known as pups) left over from other projects and welded together. Further details regarding the history of the pipeline can be found in NTSB, *Pacific Gas and Electric Company natural gas transmission pipeline rupture and fire, San Bruno, CA, September 9, 2010*, pipeline accident report, Washington DC, 2011, section 1.7.

12   Karau, SJ and Williams, KD, "Social loafing: a meta-analytic review and theoretical integration", *Journal of Personality and Social Psychology* 1993, 65: 681–706.

13   Snook, SA, *Friendly fire: the accidental shootdown of US Black Hawks over Northern Iraq*, Princeton University Press, Princeton, New Jersey, 2000, p 135.

14   Doorn, N and Van de Poel, I, "Editors' overview: moral responsibility in technology and engineering", *Science and Engineering Ethics* 2012, 18: 1–11.

15   Although taking an organisational view of accidents (as described in Chapter 1), we would argue that allocation of blame is a different question entirely.

Chapter

3

16   CPUC, *Rebuttal testimony of Raffy Stepanian*, CPUC, Consumer Protection & Safety Division, San Francisco, 20 August 2012, p 36. Available at ftp://ftp.cpuc.ca.gov/SanBrunoReports/CPSD%20Reply%20Testimony.pdf.

17   Hopkins, A, *Failure to learn: the BP Texas City Refinery disaster*, CCH Australia Limited, Sydney, 2008.

CHAPTER 4

THE MARSHALL AND GULF OF MEXICO OIL SPILLS

Decision-making immediately prior to the Enbridge accident was flawed in a variety of ways. As we studied these flaws, we were struck by the fact that they were the very same flaws we had identified in the decision-making process immediately prior to the BP Gulf of Mexico blowout.[1] Accordingly, we decided to write this chapter as a systematic comparison between the two. The basic structure of much of the chapter will be to identify a flaw, illustrate it by reference to the Gulf of Mexico accident, and then demonstrate how it affected decision-making in the Enbridge case. The chapter concludes with some suggestions on how these flaws might be avoided.

Two competing paradigms are used when discussing the flawed decision-making of frontline personnel, one normative and the other explanatory. The normative paradigm attributes accidents to individual fault, with those at fault deserving some kind of censure. In contrast, the explanatory paradigm asks why the person behaved as he or she did, which takes us into the realm of human and organisational factors. Often, the same behaviour can be viewed in either or both ways. The main aim of this chapter is explanatory but, to clear the decks, we begin with some remarks about the normative approach.

The normative approach

Carelessness

One of the most common normative judgments after an accident is that the people concerned were careless, meaning they did not exercise the degree of care that they *ought* to have exercised. Hence, the outcome is their fault. Where carelessness is seen as the cause, the response of companies is often to urge workers to be more careful, a predictably futile strategy. The fact is that identifying carelessness as a cause provides no useful guidance on how to prevent accidents.

There is a legal counterpart to carelessness. At law, behaviour is negligent if the person concerned did not exercise the level of care that a "reasonable person" would have exercised in the circumstances. A finding of negligence is thus a finding of carelessness. From this point of view, courts are powerful reinforcers of the popular tendency to see carelessness as the cause of accidents. It is noteworthy that two of the men involved in the flawed decision-making prior to the Gulf of Mexico accident were charged with criminal negligence.[2] However, as we will see in this chapter, their mistakes were entirely explicable in terms of several well-known social psychological mechanisms. From this point of view, it is wholly inappropriate to blame them. There has been a particular tendency to criminalise hospital personnel and, in some countries, airline pilots whose mistakes have proved fatal.[3] In nearly all cases, however, this is just as inappropriate as criminalising the mistakes of the frontline decision-makers in the Gulf of Mexico blowout.

Incompetence

Although "carelessness" is generally out of favour with accident analysts, two other normative evaluations often take its place — incompetence and complacency. Dealing first with incompetence, it is often found in accident investigations that workers did not have the necessary competence to do the job they were doing. This is a factual statement, not a normative judgment. Moreover, there are practical preventive measures that follow, for instance, better training and better auditing of competence. However, a subtle transformation often takes place: the problem is not just lack of the necessary competence; the problem is that the workers were "incompetent". Here we are dealing with the subtleties of the English language, and we need to be aware of these subtleties to understand how normative judgments creep in. "Competence" is a noun, referring to a particular human attribute. Moreover, "the necessary competence" is a qualified or limited component of the sum total of competencies that a person may have. To say that the worker lacked the necessary competence is obviously not a judgment about the whole person. "Incompetent", on the other hand, is an adjective, and when it qualifies "worker", it becomes an all-encompassing statement about that person. It is akin to a normative evaluation in that there is an unspoken implication that the incompetence is the fault of the worker concerned. This assumption is necessarily unspoken because it could not survive rational scrutiny. One tell-tale indicator of this normative element is that, when "incompetent" is used in spoken language, the tone often conveys disgust or exasperation, and sometimes even ridicule. In this way, a factual statement becomes a normative evaluation, possibly without the speaker even realising. A striking example of this is contained in the press statement by the chair of the National Transportation Safety Board (NTSB) at the time of the release of its report into the Enbridge accident:

> "This investigation identified a complete breakdown of safety at Enbridge. Their employees performed like Keystone Cops and failed to recognize their pipeline had ruptured and continued to pump crude into the environment."

The Keystone Cops were comically incompetent policemen who featured in silent films in the early part of the 20th century. They were objects of ridicule. When making this comparison, the chair of the NTSB was ridiculing the mistakes of the Enbridge employees. The NTSB report itself did no such thing, but the comments of its chair reveal how easily we can slip into being judgmental about those who make mistakes.

Complacency

The third example of this kind of judgment is "complacency". The regulatory inquiry that followed the Gulf of Mexico accident concluded that "overall complacency of the [rig] crew was a possible contributing cause ... of the blowout". Interestingly, a few months earlier on another rig, the same rig owner had suffered a very similar blowout, which was fortunately arrested before it got out of control. It was in fact a frightening near miss. The company's response was to admonish its employees in an advisory email: "Do not be complacent ... remain focused." It is clear from this statement that the company regarded the behaviour of its employees as blameworthy. Their "complacent" behaviour was their fault.

However, so-called complacent behaviour is learned behaviour. Workers may learn that it is safe to take a particular short cut, to ignore a particular defence, since, in their experience, other defences can be relied on. To describe such behaviour as complacent entirely misses the point: practical experience has taught them to behave in this way. Practical experience — trial and error learning — is one of the most influential of teachers, far more influential in many circumstances than theoretical knowledge. Unfortunately, though, when dealing with catastrophic events, trial and error learning is not appropriate. Relevant learning opportunities are few and far between and, in any case, the consequences are too serious to allow people to learn from their own mistakes. In these circumstances, organisations must make strenuous efforts to *counteract* on-the-job learning. Simply to condemn the behaviour as complacent is predictably futile.*

Explanation

Consider now the explanatory approach. This seeks not to allocate blame, but to understand why people made the decisions they made. The approach starts from the presumption that decision-makers thought they were doing the right thing at the time. The puzzle is: how is it that well-intentioned and intelligent people can get it so wrong? The answer is that a powerful set of social and psychological forces is often at work, predisposing them to make the wrong decisions.**

---

* A fourth explanation of this type is "apathy". This was made famous by Lord Robens in his 1972 report on defects in existing United Kingdom health and safety legislation: "We suggested at the outset that apathy is the greatest single contributing factor to accidents at work." Quoted in Cullen, WD, *The public inquiry into the Piper Alpha disaster*, HMSO, London, 1990, p 256.

** Interestingly, the International Association of Oil and Gas Producers (OGP) identified a similar set of "cognitive issues" in a recent report: OGP, *Cognitive issues associated with process safety and environmental incidents*, report no. 460, 2012.

The decisions

In order to explore the social and psychological forces at work, we need to know more about the decisions that were in fact made.

In the case of the BP oil well, the rig crew had just completed drilling the well. They had struck oil and gas and now had to seal the bottom of the well with a cement plug, so that the rig could move on to its next job. This was intended to be a temporary measure: at some later date, the well would be connected to other infrastructure and brought into production. The oil and gas at the bottom of the well was under high pressure, and during normal drilling operations, the well was prevented from blowing out by a column of heavy drilling fluid that filled the entire well. But much of this fluid had to be removed prior to departure, at which time, the cement plug would be the primary barrier to blowout. The vital question, then, was: could the cement be relied on? Had the well been effectively sealed? To answer this question, the team carried out an "integrity" test. They experimentally reduced the pressure in the well by removing some of the drilling fluid and replacing it with seawater. Assuming that the cement plug was working, nothing should happen. In fact, the pressure in the well began to rise, indicating unequivocally that the well was not sealed and would blow out as soon as circumstances permitted. However, the team that carried out the test misinterpreted the results and concluded that the well was secure. This mistaken conclusion will be analysed shortly.

In the case of the Enbridge pipeline, a section of pipe running though the state of Michigan ruptured due to inadequate maintenance (to be discussed in Chapter 5). The pipeline was operated from a control room in Edmonton, Alberta, and at the time, operators were shutting down flow as part of a routine procedure. Alarms went off in the Alberta control room but the operators did not recognise them for what they were. A relatively small amount of dilbit (diluted bitumen) was released at this stage. Hours later, operators tried to restart the line. Alarms again went off but the operators did not respond and continued pumping for an hour before they stopped, perplexed that they had not been able to re-establish flow at a point downstream from where, unbeknown to them, the line had ruptured. During this time, a large amount of dilbit was pumped out into a nearby river system. Two hours later, the operators tried again and pumped for half an hour, ignoring alarms. They were considering a third attempt to restart when word came through that a massive release had taken place.

Normalisation of warning signs

In both of the above cases, employees misinterpreted what should have been clear indicators of danger. The way they were able to do this was by providing an alternative interpretation of these indicators which enabled them to "normalise" the warnings they were receiving.

Normalisation is a mental process that has been found to play a role in many accidents. The best-known account of this phenomenon is provided by sociologist Diane Vaughan[4] in her discussion of the space shuttle *Challenger*, which caught fire and plunged to earth in 1986, killing the seven astronauts on board. The integrity of the booster rockets depended on certain rubber seals, known as O-rings. It had been discovered on several previous shuttle launches that they did not perform as required at low temperatures. Indeed, they malfunctioned. Nevertheless, they had not failed totally. Over time, this partial malfunction was reconceptualised as normal, and the risk of total failure came to be judged as acceptably low. Vaughan described this as the normalisation of deviance, by which she meant the normalisation of deviation, or partial malfunction, or increased risk. The temperature on the launch day was colder than at previous launches. But the technical malfunction had been normalised. The launch was thus given the go-ahead. This time, the seals failed totally, with catastrophic results. Tragically, the same process of normalisation contributed to the *Columbia* shuttle accident 17 years later,[5] although of course the technical causes were different.*

The normalisation of warning signs is a variation on this theme. It is almost always the case that major accidents are preceded by events that amount to warnings, and that, had these warnings been heeded, the accident would have been averted. For instance, four men drowned in an Australian coal mine when miners inadvertently broke through into old, abandoned workings that were full of water, as old workings often are. As mining operations approached the old workings, water began to seep out of the mine face, indicating that they were dangerously close. However, this indication of danger was dismissed on the grounds that the coal seam was naturally wet and that water seeping out of the mine face was therefore to be expected. In other words, the water was explained away as normal.[6]

The problem is that warning signs may have multiple interpretations, at least one of which is benign. If a benign interpretation can be identified, this can be used to explain away the warning. The anomaly is no longer an anomaly; it is what would be expected in the circumstances; it is normal. This is what happened at the Australian mine. It is also what happened in the two cases under discussion here.

---

* The best operational managers in hazardous industries are acutely aware of the phenomenon of normalisation. They know that, if one of several controls that are supposed to be in place is not working, the risk of failure may only be marginally greater and the increased risk is therefore tolerable for a short period. They also know that the longer this situation is allowed to persist, the greater the likelihood that it will come to be regarded as normal. They therefore devise rules for themselves to guard against this possibility. In one reported case, managers would draw "a line in the sand" for themselves: if the problem was not fixed by a certain deadline, the plant would be taken out of operation until it was. Hayes, J, *Operational decision-making in high-hazard organizations: drawing a line in the sand*, Ashgate, Farnham, 2013.

Normalising the warnings of blowout
Our first question then is: how did the decision-making team on the drilling rig normalise or explain away the rise in pressure? They did so by invoking a "bladder effect". It is not possible in this brief account to describe how the bladder effect was supposed to operate.[7] Suffice it to say that it purported to explain the rising pressure that the team was seeing.

The decision-making team consisted of drillers who were employees of the rig owner, Transocean, and two BP company representatives who were stationed on the rig to supervise drilling operations. The bladder theory was propounded by the drillers who said that they had seen this phenomenon before when doing tests of this nature and that it was not uncommon. The BP men had not heard of it, but found themselves persuaded by the logic. However, according to all the experts, the bladder effect makes no sense and could not possibly account for the findings. The original proponents of the theory died in the accident, so it has not been possible to explore the origins of the theory.

In the cold light of hindsight, the bladder effect has no credibility, but it was sufficiently convincing on the day to serve as an ad hoc explanation for the unexpected pressure readings being observed. In this way, what should have been an unequivocal warning was normalised.

Normalising the spill alarms
A similar process of normalisation was at work in the Enbridge case. The alarm system was based on pressure variations, and on the occasion in question, alarms were triggered by a drop in line pressure downstream of the rupture. However, operators had available to them a second, benign explanation of why they were getting alarms warning of an oil spill — "column separation". This is a real phenomenon. In certain circumstances, the column of liquid in the pipeline may separate, leaving the intervening space occupied by a bubble of vapour. Where column separation has occurred, operators can pump liquid in at one end without seeing any increase in pressure at the other, since the input liquid is presumed to be filling up the cavity. Only after the cavity is filled and the liquid is flowing again through the whole line will a rise in pressure at one end be matched by a rise in pressure at the other. Column separation is most likely when a pipeline runs up or down hill. The area where the spill occurred was relatively flat and historical data showed that column separation was rare in the Michigan pipeline. Nevertheless, column separation provided an alternative explanation for the pressure alarms being seen.

Confirmation bias
Although personnel had alternative explanations to hand for the anomalies they were seeing, there remains the question of why they so readily discarded the more

worrying interpretations. Part of the reason is that both groups were subject to profound confirmation bias. "Confirmation bias" is a well-known psychological phenomenon that refers to the preference people have for information that confirms rather than disconfirms their beliefs. It is an unconscious process, not a deliberate attempt to build a one-sided case.[8] Teams carrying out risk assessments are renowned for this kind of bias. Where a particular course of action is being considered, teams will frequently make selective use of information suggesting that the risk is acceptably low and discard or fail to consider information that suggests otherwise.

Confirmation bias in the BP well integrity test

Why did the decision-making team carrying out the well integrity test so readily adopt the bladder theory? The answer is that, hours earlier, on the basis of incomplete evidence, the engineers had declared that the cement job was a success. Indeed, they were so confident that they abandoned another test procedure which they had planned to use if they had any doubts about the success of the cement job. All this would have powerfully reinforced the confirmation bias of the people engaged in the well integrity test. The purpose of the test in their minds was not to *investigate* whether the well was sealed, but to *confirm* that it was. It was therefore necessary to find an alternative interpretation of the anomalous results and to continue testing until this confirmation was forthcoming. The Presidential Commission that investigated the accident puts it well:[9]

> "[The testers] began with the assumption that the cement job had been successful and kept running tests and proposing explanations until they convinced themselves that their assumption was correct."

Confirmation bias in the Enbridge oil release

In the Enbridge case, given the relative frequencies of rupture and column separation, the most likely explanation was column separation. On that assumption, operators calculated that it would take 20 minutes of pumping to reunite the column and to see the pressure rise at the other end. In fact, they pumped for an hour without any discernible effect on the downstream pressure, at which point they stopped, baffled. However, even at this stage, they did not reconsider their explanation. An analyst in the group explained that the problem must be "*severe* column separation", in this way rescuing the theory. Accordingly, they pumped for another half hour, still without effect. At last they began to doubt their explanation and to wonder if in fact there was a leak. They contacted the Chicago area manager for the company who said that he had had no reports of spills in the area and that he was in favour of trying again. This tipped the balance back in favour of the column separation theory and operators were about to try again when they received a call notifying them of a major spill. Finally, they were forced to recognise what had happened. But the fact that they had stuck to their theory despite mounting evidence of its inadequacy demonstrates the power of the confirmation bias to which they were subject.

Situational awareness

The concept of situational awareness has become a popular way of understanding mistakes made by operators in complex environments — in particular, mistakes made by aircraft pilots.[10] Pilots have, on occasion, crashed aircraft because they did not know where they were, and sometimes because they did not even realise they were descending. Where people have wrong or inadequate mental models of the situation they are in, decision-making can prove disastrous. A relevant example in the present context is the case of BP operators who overfilled the distillation column at the Texas City Refinery in 2005, initiating a disastrous explosion. These operators had an erroneous mental model of the situation, believing that that column was nearly empty, when in fact it was nearly full. Their erroneous understanding of the situation stemmed largely from the lack of appropriate instrumentation which would have drawn attention to the level in the column.

The Gulf of Mexico well integrity test required the rig team to substitute sea water for the drilling fluid in a section of the well that was more than 1.5 km below sea level, creating in effect a water-filled cavity at that point. Two small diameter pipes tapped into this cavity and ran to the surface. The pressure at the top of these pipes should have been identical, no matter what. It wasn't: the reading at the top of one pipe was high, while the reading at the top of the other was zero. The only conclusion that could be drawn from this was that there was something wrong with the test set-up itself. But the team did not draw this conclusion. They decided that the high reading on one pipe was a result of the bladder effect, while the zero reading on the other was the true value, indicating that the well was sealed. This conclusion revealed an entirely inadequate mental model of what they were doing — a complete lack of situational awareness.

Similarly, the Enbridge operators pumped oil into a presumed column separation which they had initially calculated would take 20 minutes to fill. After that 20 minutes had passed, they continued pumping with no idea of the cause or extent of what they now presumed to be *severe* column separation. Their actions revealed no awareness of the situation they were in. In this respect, there was a marked similarity between their decision-making and that of the crew engaged in the well integrity test.

The decision-making process: inappropriate deference to presumed expertise

Yet another similarity concerned the decision-making process itself. In both cases, certain individuals had formal responsibility for making decisions but, in both cases, they deferred to others whom they presumed had greater expertise, but who in fact did not.

In the well integrity test, formal decision-making authority lay with the two BP company representatives on the rig. However, they were not experienced in carrying out integrity tests. The Transocean drillers on the other hand had long experience of such tests, and it was they who proposed and championed the bladder theory. The BP company men were at first sceptical, but in the end they deferred to the drillers.

This was not just a matter of deference to presumed expertise; it was also a manifestation of the power of the subculture of the rig. The culture of the drillers has been described as follows:[11]

Chapter

4

> "Drillers are highly skilled technicians who take a personal interest in every well. This small, tightly woven fraternity of opinionated people is very aware of their importance to the success of the project. The majority of skilled drillers are over 50 years old ...
>
> It is a leadership role, by practice if not definition ...
>
> Complexity is reflected in the seemingly unending acronyms, obscure terms freely mixed from any number of professional disciplines, and oilfield slang, add to the complex mind-set. These terms are also a means to manage the complexity. They form a sort of secret language that binds offshore workers. Complexity is also mitigated by teasing and self-deprecating, competitive humour. Peer pressure is important. No one wants to be branded a 'worm' (slang used to describe someone for asking seemingly 'dumb' questions)."

This was the culture with which the BP company men had to contend. They were not associated with the rig long term, but came and went. Indeed, on this occasion, one of the two company men had been on the rig for only a few days.

At first, only one of the BP men accepted the bladder theory, leaving the other as the sole hold-out — the one person blocking consensus. This was clearly a difficult situation for him to be in. What made it worse was that, as he told BP interviewers, the "drillers found it humorous" that he was uncomfortable with their explanation.[12] One can infer from this that they were "teasing" him, to use the language quoted above. This was the culture of the drillers in action — in this case, aimed at bringing not just one of their own into line, but the BP company man himself.

In the end, the dominant members of the group prevailed. This was a classic example of groupthink, in which doubters in a decision-making group are silenced by the more powerful members of the group.[13] So it was that the two company men deferred to the presumed expertise of the drillers and formally declared that the test had been successful.

In the Enbridge case, decision-making authority lay with the operator on duty. If necessary, decisions would be escalated to a team leader, or even a supervisor, who was either on location or on call. In addition, operators could call on the assistance of a material balance analyst, who analysed in- and out-flows at various points in the pipeline and determined whether they were in balance. If they were not, this might indicate a column separation or a leak. These material balance analysts were the "experts" on whom the operators and their supervisors relied. Whether they should have relied on the analysts in this way is a moot point. In the simulator training they received, operators were required to make decisions without input from material balance analysts. Moreover, material balance analysts were trained to provide their results to operators with a warning that the results were not reliable when a column separation was present and that operators should make their own decision about whether to start pumping. There was certainly no requirement that analysts make a determination of whether an alarm was true or false. From this point of view, the operator on duty should not have simply deferred to the advice of the material balance analyst.

However, in apparent contradiction of the procedures written for *analysts*, the procedures for *operators* required them to ascertain from the analysts whether an alarm was true or false, and to act on that information. Furthermore, it seems that the analysts were ready to go along with the operators' expectations and offer a view as to whether an alarm was true or false. In short, the operators put the analysts in a de facto decision-making role which the analysts accepted. The official report on the accident made the following comment about this:[14]

> "The NTSB has investigated previous accidents in which breakdowns in team performance occurred. In these accidents, team leaders transferred their authority to subordinates who they believed possessed more expertise than they did in the circumstances they were encountering …
>
> [In the Enbridge] accident, the assigned leader of the team (the on-call supervisor) deferred his authority to the … analyst. The two individuals essentially reversed roles."

While the NTSB report is correct in treating this as an example of deference to a presumed expert, the fact that some of the procedures also required operators to do just that, contrary to their training, provides some vindication for the operators and their supervisors. It also raises questions about how such contradictory procedures came to be written. Perhaps they were no more than codifications of what operators in fact did, as procedures sometimes are, in which case, they are a consequence of the operators' tendency to defer to presumed experts, not a cause. The official report does not provide any information on this point.

A culture of casual compliance

One of the abiding findings of accident investigations is that workers routinely fail to comply with relevant procedures. For instance, this was one of the findings of the investigation into the explosion at the Texas City Refinery in 2005. Indeed, prior to that explosion, managers recognised that the site had a culture of "casual compliance", meaning that people treated procedures as guidelines only, which could be ignored whenever they had reason to do so.[15]

This analysis does not apply to the well integrity test since there were no relevant procedures to be followed. Indeed, that was one of the factors that allowed things to go so disastrously wrong. This is not to say that staff on the drilling rig generally complied with procedures where they existed. There were plenty of examples that came to light in the inquiries where that was not the case. However, procedural non-compliance was not at the heart of the failure of the well integrity test.

Chapter

4

The failure to comply with procedures was certainly a feature of the Enbridge accident. The NTSB speaks of a "culture of deviance", a "culture that accepted not adhering to the procedures". One example stands out — the 10-minute rule. This required operators to stop pumping if alarms could be not be resolved within 10 minutes. The rule had been introduced after a pipeline rupture nearly two decades earlier, where operators had ignored alarms and continued to pump oil into a rupture for more than an hour before they realised what had happened. Had the operators in 2010 complied with this rule, the scale of the release would have been much less. It turns out that operators were accustomed to exceeding the 10-minute restriction, indicating that the non-compliance on this occasion was the norm, not the exception. It is that which entitles us to speak of a *culture* of deviance or non-compliance.

Summary

Let us summarise the argument to this point. There were numerous causes of the Gulf of Mexico Blowout and of the Marshall oil spill. In both cases, it is possible to identify failures that are quite remote from those discussed here, about which one can say, had they been different, the accident would not have occurred. Moreover, in both cases, it is possible to trace lines of causation back to management failures. However, in each case, the focus here has been on one critical decision-making process: in the case of the blowout, decision-making about the well integrity test, and in the Enbridge case, decision-making about whether to start pumping again.

These decision-making processes were remarkably similar, displaying the well-known problems of normalisation, confirmation bias, inadequate situational awareness, and team decision-making processes that involved deference of the formal decision-makers to the presumed expertise of subordinates. In the case of the well integrity test, this deference to the presumed expertise of others was driven by a process of groupthink, while in the Enbridge case, it was facilitated by contradictory procedures. Finally, the Enbridge accident revealed a culture of procedural non-compliance; there was no such culture in evidence in the well integrity test, in part because there were no procedures to be complied with. The fact that there were such striking similarities in how this disastrous decision-making occurred suggests that the pattern identified may well be widespread. Moreover, the factors identified are basic social and psychological processes. In a sense, we are dealing here with human nature. It is no use, therefore, berating people for such behaviour, or exhorting them to behave differently. A more fundamental approach is necessary. The last sections of this chapter will outline some possible solutions.

Possible solutions

Procedure writing

Inadequate or contradictory procedures are implicated in many accidents and we need to think carefully about how to ensure that procedures are appropriate. Sometimes procedures are written by the operators who use them, and simply codify what they already do. As a consequence, inadequate practices may end up being enshrined in writing. Alternatively, someone drafts procedures from first principles; the draft is circulated to relevant people for comment; suggestions are incorporated; and the procedure is promulgated. Sometimes suggestions are incorporated without consideration as to whether they are consistent with rest of the procedures. Moreover, defects in the original draft may not be identified. The problem is that no one, neither the drafter nor the individuals to whom the draft procedures are circulated, is truly responsible for ensuring overall consistency and workability when procedures are developed in this way — in effect, by committee. One is reminded of the process by which Bills are stitched together to secure passage through the US Congress. In order to ensure the votes of particular members of Congress, provisions may be added that do not reflect the dominant purpose of the Bill and may even be contrary to that purpose. What is needed when developing procedures is a single guiding mind, a procedure owner, who will take responsibility for every aspect of the procedures or system of procedures to ensure that they function as intended. Of course, such a person must seek the views of all of those affected by the procedure. However, in the end, one person must sign off, not merely on the fact that the necessary input has been solicited, but also that the procedure is valid.

Compliance with procedures

It cannot and must not be assumed that people will automatically comply with procedures. Here we take as our text the words of Lord Cullen in his report on the worst ever accident in the petroleum industry, the Piper Alpha disaster that claimed the lives of 167 people a quarter of a century ago:[16]

> "Over time there is an increasing probability that the procedure in practice will have departed from that originally laid down. Monitoring is required to pick this up in a timely way. It is then necessary for management to decide whether the system should be modified in the light of the perceived departures or whether additional training is required to ensure operation as originally intended."

What Lord Cullen is saying is that a culture of deviance is *to be expected, in the normal course of events,* unless active steps are taken to ensure compliance. (Lord Cullen speaks of "monitoring"; we shall use this term interchangeably with "auditing", although in some contexts, it is useful to distinguish the two.)

According to Lord Cullen, if monitoring reveals non-compliance, there are at least two possible causes:

(1) the procedures are appropriate and operators need additional training or supervision to ensure compliance; or

(2) the procedures are problematic and may need to be modified.

The second possibility requires a procedure modification process that takes account of not only the problems experienced by operators, but also the basic intent of the procedures. In other words, there must be input into this process, not only from operators, but also from the engineers who designed the procedures in the first place.

In addition, Lord Cullen recommends that critical procedures should be reviewed annually as to their overall design to ensure that they are capable of achieving their intended purpose.

There are clearly resource implications to these recommendations that must be faced if they are to be implemented.

Beyond all this lies the idea of sceptical auditing. Auditors can easily fall victim to confirmation bias, seeking evidence to confirm that operators are in compliance, rather than evidence to the contrary. It is easy enough to find evidence of compliance — paperwork is up to date, casual observation of whatever is being done at the time of the auditor's visit, and so on. The sceptical auditor, however, will identify situations where there is a particular risk that procedures will not be followed, and monitor what is in fact happening. We know that start-up and shutdown procedures are frequently violated, so the sceptical auditor will seek to audit compliance with such procedures. The problem is that start-up and shutdown are intermittent events and may occur at odd times, 4 o'clock in the morning, for instance. This means that sceptical auditors will need to put themselves out in order to be able to audit such behaviour effectively. They will need to follow a timetable that is dictated by operational considerations, not by their own convenience. This complicates the auditor's job enormously. Sometimes, the actions of operators are recorded electronically and it may be possible to study this record, after the event, to establish what was going on. Take, for example, the Texas City Refinery disaster, triggered by a start-up in which operators did not follow procedures.[17] After the accident, investigators discovered from the electronic record that operators had routinely violated procedures in previous start-ups. But management had not availed itself of this opportunity to discover what was going on. Unless auditors find ways of studying what people are actually doing, they can and should have no confidence that procedures are being followed.

We will say more about procedures in Chapter 10.

Counteracting confirmation bias

Confirmation bias results in people seeking out information that supports their preferred view and dismissing information that challenges it. In the present context, the preferred view is that the situation is under control and that operations can continue as usual, while the challenge to that view comes from the warnings and anomalies that, if taken seriously, might require operations to be stopped. In this context, then, confirmation bias involves a preference for business as usual.

This is a thought process that must be turned on its head. Where warnings and anomalies are identified, workers must assume the worst, until the contrary can be established.

This alternative mindset can be proceduralised in some circumstances. For instance, in some industries, many of the anomalous events that constitute warnings of danger can be specified. It can then be made mandatory to report these events into incident reporting systems, as in the aviation industry. Furthermore, no single anomaly may be enough to justify stopping work, but an accumulation of them may indeed justify this outcome. It may be possible to set up a rule that, when more than two or three specified anomalous events occur, certain precautionary responses are mandatory.[18] Interestingly, such a rule had been developed for the Enbridge operators, but this was one of the procedures for which compliance was treated as optional.[19]

Beyond this, companies can set up systems to acknowledge people who report and act on anomalous events.[20] This is probably the most effective way to create a real change in mindset, a real alertness and willingness to respond to warnings of danger.

Decision-making processes to counteract confirmation bias[21]

Decision-makers at all levels are subject to confirmation bias — in particular, a tendency to ignore warnings and to proceed with business as usual. Given this fact, it is important that organisations develop decision-making processes that challenge this tendency.

There is a preliminary point to be made here. In practice, much decision-making is diffuse and consensual. In such circumstances, no single person is truly accountable for the final decision. Many companies therefore promote single-point accountability for decisions, on the assumption that it makes for more responsible decision-making. This does not mean that decision-makers should act in isolation. They of course need to consult, but consultation must be kept conceptually distinct from decision-making. In principle, the decision-maker must withdraw from consultation mode before making the decision.

To combat confirmation bias, those involved in the consultation process should be encouraged to challenge any proposed course of action and to make diary notes of whatever advice they give. The manager should sign off on these notes and then make an independent decision. Challenge will only occur if people feel that they can offer opposing views without risking career-ending transfers. So the real test of this approach is whether opposing views are indeed proffered and noted. When even one person in the group is offering advice that runs counter to the proposed course of action, decision-making is likely to be more considered because the decision-maker will need to be able to provide reasons as to why it is appropriate to override the dissenting view.[22] This process can be workshopped in company training sessions so that it runs smoothly. Everyone must see it as a norm to be held to account for their views and their decisions in this way. The resulting written record will be useful for later performance reviews.

Of course, not all management decisions need to be made in this way. There must therefore be rules for deciding when decisions are sufficiently critical to justify this process, with all its attendant documentation.

For some decisions, a second and more a more elaborate challenge process is desirable. Organisations should establish a cell that acts similarly to an audit unit, answerable to senior management and available to local managers, to perform as a "red team". This concept is used in military training. A blue team (our team) devises a military strategy, and exercises are held in which the red team (the enemy) probes and tests for weaknesses. The purpose is to identify problems so that they can be corrected prior to the strategy being used in earnest.

In the present context, the red team is a multidisciplinary team whose task is to test the proposals/decisions of local managers. Its aim is to find the problems, not to endorse the proposal/decision. It must not be seen as a witch-hunter, but as a valid organisational tool. It should include relevant technical specialists, as well as people with practical experience — no more than about five in total. Organisations sometimes engage outside consultants to perform this function.[23],* The proposal here is that they create *internal* processes to challenge important decisions.

Conclusion

This chapter has been about the contribution of flawed decision-making by frontline operational staff to the Marshall accident and to the Gulf of Mexico accident. We imagine that similar flaws played a role in the San Bruno accident, although the story of that decision-making process is not on the public record. The fact is that the social psychological processes we identified are ubiquitous and can be expected to corrupt decision-making unless stringent efforts are made to ensure that they don't. The final sections of this chapter have identified some possible solutions. Companies would do well to consider these suggestions carefully; accidents will continue to happen until these human factors are taken seriously.

Endnotes

1   Hopkins, A, *Disastrous decisions: the human and organisational causes of the Gulf of Mexico blowout*, CCH Australia Limited, Sydney, 2012.

2   These charges had not come to court at the time of writing.

3   Dekker, S, *Just culture: balancing safety and accountability*, Ashgate, Aldershot, 2007.

4   Vaughan, D, *The Challenger launch decision: risky technology, culture and deviance at NASA*, University of Chicago Press, Chicago, 1996.

5   CAIB, report, vol 1, National Aeronautics and Space Administration, 2003.

6   Hopkins, A, "A culture of denial: sociological similarities between the Moura and Gretley mine disasters", *Journal of Occupational Health and Safety — Australia and New Zealand* 2000, 16(1): 29–36.

7   For a more detailed account, see:

     Hopkins, A, *Disastrous decisions: the human and organisational causes of the Gulf of Mexico blowout*, CCH Australia Limited, Sydney, 2012, p 43.

     National Commission on the BP Deepwater Horizon Oil Spill and Offshore Drilling, *Macondo: the Gulf oil disaster, Chief Counsel's report*, Washington, 2011, p 157.

8   Nickerson, R, "Confirmation bias: a ubiquitous phenomenon in many guises", *Review of General Psychology* 1998, 2: 175–220 at 175.

9   National Commission on the BP Deepwater Horizon Oil Spill and Offshore Drilling, *Macondo: the Gulf oil disaster, Chief Counsel's report*, Washington, 2011, p 161.

10   Hudson, P and van der Graaf, GC, *The rule of three: situation awareness in hazardous situations*, SPE 46765, Society of Petroleum Engineers International Conference on Health, Safety, and

---

*   Ideally, regulators in mature safety case regimes provide this kind of challenge. See Hopkins, A, *Explaining safety case*, working paper 87, National Research Centre for OHS Regulation, Canberra, 2013. Available at http://regnet.anu.edu.au/publications/wp-87-explaining-%E2%80%9Csafety-case%E2%80%9D.

Environment in Oil and Gas Exploration and Production, Caracas, Venezuela, 7 to 10 June 1998.

Flin, R, O'Connor, P and Crichton, M, *Safety at the sharp end: a guide to non-technical skills*, Ashgate, Aldershot, 2008, pp 18–19.

Salmon, PM, Stanton, NA and Young, KL, "Situation awareness on the road: review, theoretical and methodological issues, and future directions", *Theoretical Issues in Ergonomics Science* 2012, 13: 472–492.

Sneddon, A, Mearns, K and Flin, R, "Stress, fatigue, situation awareness and safety in offshore drilling crews", *Safety Science* 2013, 56: 80–88.

11   Donley, P, *This is not about mystics: or why a little science would help a lot*, Deepwater Horizon study group working paper, 2011, pp 11, 18.

12   National Commission on the BP Deepwater Horizon Oil Spill and Offshore Drilling, *Macondo: the Gulf oil disaster, Chief Counsel's report*, Washington, 2011, p 158.

13   Janis, I, *Groupthink: psychological studies of policy decisions and fiascos*, Houghton Mifflin, Boston, 1982.

14   NTSB, *Enbridge Incorporated hazardous liquid pipeline rupture and release, Marshall, Michigan, July 25, 2010*, pipeline accident report, Washington DC, 2012, pp 94–95.

15   Hopkins, A, *Failure to learn: the BP Texas City Refinery disaster*, CCH Australia Limited, Sydney, 2008, p 10.

16   Cullen, WD, *The public inquiry into the Piper Alpha disaster*, HMSO, London, 1990, p 294.

17   Hopkins, A, *Failure to learn: the BP Texas City Refinery disaster*, CCH Australia Limited, Sydney, 2008, p 60.

18   Hopkins, A, "Risk-management and rule-compliance: decision-making in hazardous industries", *Safety Science* 2011, 49: 110–120.

19   NTSB, *Enbridge Incorporated hazardous liquid pipeline rupture and release, Marshall, Michigan, July 25, 2010*, pipeline accident report, Washington DC, 2012, p 98.

20   Hopkins, A, *Disastrous decisions: the human and organisational causes of the Gulf of Mexico blowout*, CCH Australia Limited, Sydney, 2012, p 133.

21   This section draws heavily on conversations with Lochie McLean, a colleague with long experience in the military.

22   What is being proposed here is similar to the devil's advocate strategy, but it differs in that no one person is assigned the devil's advocate role.

23   Leveson, N, *The use of safety cases in certification and regulation*, MIT ESD technical report, 2011. Available at http://sunnyday.mit.edu/safer-world.

Chapter

4

Part 2

CHAPTER 5

INTEGRITY MANAGEMENT AND RISK ASSESSMENT

In Part 2, we move away from the relatively immediate operational causes of the San Bruno and Marshall accidents to causes that are, in some sense, more remote. In this chapter, we examine the integrity and risk assessment processes and the way that they failed. The issues are sufficiently similar that we treat the two accidents together, in the same chapter.

Both the Enbridge and PG&E pipelines failed as a result of defects in the metal body of the pipelines themselves — faulty welding in the fabrication of the pipeline in the case of PG&E and corrosion cracks in the case of Enbridge. The primary engineering function intended to prevent the failure of high-pressure pipelines due to problems such as these is known as integrity management. This is the process by which any pipeline company tries to detect and repair material defects so as to prevent pipeline leaks and the resulting impact on people, property and the environment. At PG&E, the problem with line 132 was not detected. At Enbridge, cracks in line 6B were detected but a decision was made not to repair them. It is instructive to consider why the systems designed to manage this risk failed so comprehensively in both cases.

Some threats to pipeline integrity are specific events — operating the pipeline at higher than normal pressure, or work near the pipeline that could cause damage. Such events may be identified by direct evidence such as operating records that reveal significant pressure changes, or patrolling to identify unauthorised activity near a pipeline. The challenge for companies that may be responsible for literally thousands of miles of underground pipelines is that the effects of some of the most significant threats to integrity — such as corrosion — accumulate very slowly over long periods of time. The system is weakened, but there may be few readily observable signs. The physical condition of buried pipelines and any incremental degradation is not easy to identify. Testing the integrity of lines is a costly undertaking, even before any repairs are contemplated. For this reason, prioritising engineering inspection activities that can find damaged coating, cracks, dents, pitting and the like is a task with significant cost and safety implications. In addition, there are further costs linked to the results of inspection, as decisions about further investigation and repair are required.

Balancing cost and safety is a problem faced by many hazardous industries and a common solution is to use risk, ie to consider both the likelihood and the consequences of possible accident scenarios. The pipeline industry in the United States has gone down this track, with both PG&E and Enbridge using a "risk index model" to prioritise pipeline segments for inspection. This is in contrast to other safety decisions examined in earlier chapters which were based on regulatory compliance. Since the outcomes are so important, there are several significant limitations inherent in this type of modelling and the way in which it was applied that are worthy of detailed consideration.

Using this approach to manage pipeline integrity raises several key questions, such as:

- How does this system deal with absolute risk? How do you know if you are spending enough?
- What does the overall risk score really mean?
- Is this an effective way of planning inspection activity?
- When problems are identified in inspections, how are decisions made on whether repairs are needed?

These issues are addressed in turn below.

Spending enough

Risk index modelling as used in the US pipeline industry is about risk ranking, not absolute risk. A stated key purpose of the modelling is to determine the best allocation of the available inspection budget. As PG&E's Director of Integrity Management told the National Transportation Safety Board (NTSB), "so when we calculate the risk … it's for the establishment of the scheduling of the work".[1] This assumes that there is an adequate budget allocated to do the necessary work and the primary goal of risk management is to establish spending priorities within it. Similarly, Enbridge documentation says that "risk can be controlled through cost-effective application of finite resources".[2]

This is true in that successfully mitigating operational risks does not require an infinite budget, but pipeline risk is dynamic, increasing as facilities age and corrode. Risk will also vary with changes to the types of activities undertaken near the pipeline by landowners, other industries and the public. The budget required to ensure that risk is controlled to an acceptable level depends on the level of risk and cannot be determined independently. Both PG&E and Enbridge seem to be suggesting that risk in their systems can be adequately controlled simply by the best allocation of the resources that the organisation chooses to make available for that purpose in any given year. This is a major assumption and yet it goes unstated and so untested and unverified.

This approach to the allocation of resources is sometimes linked to quality management concepts of continuous improvement. In this way of thinking about performance improvement, the system is critically examined in the highest risk areas. Improvements are identified and then changes made, so the overall risk is thought to be declining. This can be a seriously misleading assumption because it is only true if the improvements made are adequate to offset any other changes to the system that are causing risk to increase (such as corrosion). If the system is corroding faster than repairs are being made, then the program may be slowing the rate at which risk is increasing, rather than making a reduction in risk in absolute terms. Such are the problems of risk management in a dynamic system — organisations that fail to take this effect into account may not be preventing accidents but simply slowly managing their facilities to failure. Of course, corrosion, fatigue and other natural processes leading to the need for repair are also unlikely to be identified in neat time periods that follow the annual budget cycles of most management processes. Spending to keep the system safe is almost bound to require "lumpy" spending patterns, rather than uniform annual budget allocations.

We now return to the risk index approach as implemented at PG&E and Enbridge. Since the absolute risk level is not considered, the total budget made available for inspection (for example) is not driven by risk, but by other external factors such as cost and overall company profitability. It is not hard to see that this way of managing risk is unsustainable if spending is not adequate, and without considering absolute risk, there is no way of knowing how much spending is enough. If one takes the alternative, absolute view of risk, the first requirement is to determine the level of risk that is acceptable. This will determine the budget that needs to be allocated to achieve the necessary risk reduction. Principles of continuous improvement only operate when the absolute risk level is within reasonable bounds. If the risk is too high, then additional resources *must* be found. This type of approach to risk is the basis of safety regulation in Europe and Australia and will be discussed further in Chapter 9.

Determining risk in absolute terms is difficult to do with a high degree of accuracy. Nevertheless, the question cannot be avoided. By not addressing this issue directly, both PG&E and Enbridge were making the assumption that the risk posed by their pipeline network was, at the very least, not unacceptably high. Any well thought out risk management system must be able to test that assumption without waiting for a major failure to highlight that it is not true. This is especially important in a general environment of cost pressures in many organisations. Cost-cutting or minimising expenditure has been found to be a significant factor in several recent major accidents, including cutting maintenance budgets at the BP Texas City Refinery before the serious fire at that site,[3] cancelling critical well integrity testing before the *Deepwater Horizon* blowout,[4]

Chapter

5

and changes to well integrity systems to minimise costs before the Montara blowout.[5] As we will discuss in Chapter 8, there is direct evidence that PG&E also fell into this trap.

Overall scores

The risk index approach used by both PG&E and Enbridge relies on any pipeline system being divided into a possibly very large number of segments.[6] The overall premise of the approach is that the risk posed by each pipeline segment can be determined relative to others. In this way, a ranked list of segments is produced which can then be used to prioritise inspection activities. The relative risk score is based on both the potential impact of a leak and the known and imagined threats to the integrity of the segment. The impact and each identified threat are then individually scored based on a set of identified attributes that are believed to affect risk (either positively or negatively). Scores are then combined to develop a risk index for each segment. This approach is shown in Figure 5.1.[7]

The overall risk score for each segment is composed of several individual indices. The leak impact factor characterises the consequences of pipeline failure. Conceptually, this is relatively straightforward, taking into account possible impacts on people, property and the environment. The more difficult aspect to assess is the likelihood of a leak. This is done by determining threats to pipeline integrity. The standard method suggests that four threat indices are appropriate — third-party damage, corrosion, design and incorrect operations.[7]

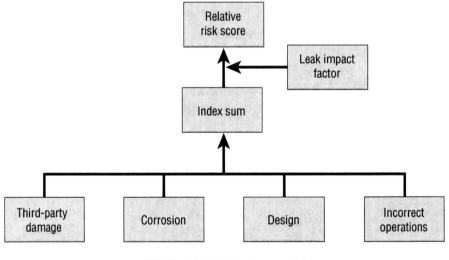

FIGURE 5.1: Risk index model

A key advantage of using such a risk-based approach to inspection management is that, in theory at least, it allows an "apples with apples" comparison. By generating a single risk score for each segment, all of the various known integrity issues are evaluated on a common footing so that decisions can be made on a logical basis. In practice then, for a system such as this to be effective, we must have a clear understanding of how the outcome will be used and, in turn, the scope of the risk assessment required. This system could be used to address prioritisation of *all* risk mitigation activities, not just inspection. Indeed, the risk index model on which the PG&E system is based addresses all threats to pipeline integrity and is apparently designed to do more than simply drive inspection planning (although this is one key aspect).

PG&E's overarching risk management procedure[8] also requires the system to include all threats and to consider "all risk mitigation strategies". In addition to considering consequences, PG&E has chosen to assess the likelihood of pipeline integrity problems due to four threats — external corrosion, third-party interference, ground movement and design and materials. Despite this broad-ranging initial step, the later stages of the procedure then focus on establishing a list of segments ranked in order of risk so as to drive the company's inspection program priorities. It was also a regulatory requirement to have an inspection program driven by risk. But not all of the threats included in the PG&E model are best mitigated by inspection. Third-party interference, ie people from outside the pipeline industry potentially damaging pipelines due to unauthorised work, is best mitigated by measures such as effective signage, patrolling the pipelines, the depth of burial of the line, or providing protective concrete slabbing over the pipelines. If the purpose of the risk model is to establish inspection priorities, this should not be driven by the potential for third-party interference.

So the first issue with the overall risk scores produced by the model is the scope of the risks that are being addressed, and whether the resulting risk index is fit for the purpose for which it was being used. Bizarrely, PG&E included the potential for pipelines to be subject to third-party interference as one of four factors driving the company's inspection priorities when inspection is not a key method of controlling this risk.

The second problem with the overall risk score is the way in which the individual scores were combined. As this is quite a technical issue, we have included the details of the argument as an Appendix, but the overall problem is that, by averaging high and low risk scores for different threats together, PG&E masked rather than emphasised problems, thus making the overall score effectively meaningless.

As a result of these problems, the overall risk index actually says very little about the relative risk posed by any given segment that might be mitigated by inspection. Further, the indices can actually mask useful information. It is not hard to see therefore that basing risk management decisions on risk index sums in this way is fundamentally flawed.

Despite this major shortcoming, risk index scores can produce some useful information. Scores across different segments for one given cause of leakage *are* comparable, eg the relative scores for external corrosion give an indication of the vulnerability of each segment (within the accuracy of the index itself). One output from this exercise could be a listing of segments showing which are most vulnerable to each identified threat. On the other hand, a comparison across threats is meaningless. Total scores should not be used to establish resourcing priorities for risk control across threats, and yet this is exactly the way in which the risk index scores were used at PG&E to prioritise pipeline inspection activities.

Planning inspection work

In order to understand the choices made by PG&E regarding inspection activities, it is first necessary to explain a little about the available methods.

There are three ways in which to test or inspect a section of existing buried pipeline in order to make an assessment of its integrity. The first is hydrotesting, ie filling the pipeline with water and pressuring to a specific value for a fixed duration (based on standards for testing) to ensure that it has sufficient strength, ie it does not leak. This can be operationally complex, as the line being tested must be taken out of gas service and customers must be supplied via an alternative route. It is also important to ensure that the line is thoroughly dried before being put back into service. Changes in local geography (high points and low points) can also create challenges for testing. As a test, it is the most comprehensive because it provides a direct indication of the ability of the pipeline to withstand internal pressure, irrespective of the types of flaws that may or may not be present.

The second method of assessing integrity is in-line inspection (ILI), known as "pigging". This involves using gas pressure to push a device that can measure wall thickness (known as an "intelligent pig") through the pipeline. Results can be used to locate "anomalies" (ie local variations in the thickness of the metal) along the pipeline that need to be further physically investigated and perhaps repaired. New pipelines are usually designed to be able to be inspected by this method. Older pipelines sometimes contain tight bends, reduced bore valves and other fittings that have the potential to impede the progress of the pig along the pipeline. As a result, ILI may not be possible without making modifications to the pipeline first.

The third method of integrity assessment is another inspection method, known as direct assessment. This means digging up and physically inspecting sections of a pipeline in order to collect information about the condition of the pipeline at a specific location. In addition to visual inspection, other testing can be carried out using ultrasonic or X-ray technology or similar. It is usually the cheapest inspection method, especially for old pipelines that were not designed for ILI, but it provides only limited data — one specific location and corrosion threats to integrity only. Critically, seam defects cannot be detected in this way.[9]

It should be clear from these high-level descriptions that these methods are not equivalent.[10] The "gold standard" for pipeline integrity assessment is hydrotesting. Despite this, much of PG&E's network had never been hydrotested prior to the San Bruno accident. In the mind of the PG&E engineers (and the regulators), hydrotesting requirements seemed to be viewed as being related to setting the maximum allowable operating pressure (MAOP) only. As discussed in Chapter 3, PG&E's engineers found a way around the requirement to hydrotest the line in order to set the MAOP. The option to hydrotest was apparently dismissed at that point. There seemed to be no understanding that this method should be considered directly as part of integrity management in order to conclusively demonstrate strength and to avoid leaks. Instead, PG&E's integrity management focus was on inspection.

Only 21% of PG&E's network was suitable for ILI and so the method most commonly used for pipeline inspection was direct assessment. This was the method of choice, *irrespective of the identified threats.*[11] As described earlier, direct assessment is a method aimed at identifying problems with corrosion, and it is completely ineffective as an inspection method for other potential pipeline threats such as construction defects. One is reminded of the apocryphal story of the drunk who searched for his keys under a street light, even though that was not where he had lost them, simply because that was where it was easiest to see.[12] This means that, even if the part of line 132 that ultimately failed had been chosen for inspection, the best we can say is that visual inspection of the outside of the line should have revealed the presence of the longitudinal weld. On the other hand, the serious fault with the weld that ultimately failed was on the inside of the pipeline and was not detectable using PG&E's chosen inspection method.

As we have demonstrated, PG&E used meaningless numbers to decide which segments to inspect. Worse than this, the company chose a particular inspection method because it was cheap, rather than because it would be effective. Identified threats were not used effectively as a guide to what inspection method was needed. Under these circumstances, is it any wonder that the integrity management system failed to identify the problems with line 132?

The faulty weld

Our critique of PG&E's inspection management arrangements has one final focus — the data used to generate the individual threat scores.

The heart of the risk index model is the method used to generate the scores for individual threats. PG&E's method used a series of questions based on the physical properties of the pipeline segments, data from past inspections, and judgments about other issues deemed to be relevant to risk. The estimated 1.25 million individual pieces of information supporting ongoing pipeline integrity planning were managed by PG&E using a large database called the geographic information system (GIS). Ultimately, ongoing integrity of the system relies on knowledge about the physical pipelines — the wall thickness of the pipe, how the metal was formed into a cylinder, how deeply the line is buried, the condition of any coating, and many other properties. On the basis of this information, judgments are made about the need for further testing and inspection, and defects that remain hidden are never going to be repaired. In the San Bruno case, the description of the installed facilities was not only wrong, but it also should have been obviously wrong to an experienced technical person looking critically at the data.

The NTSB investigation found that the San Bruno pipeline was recorded in the GIS as a single section of seamless pipe. This information was incorrect. The section in question was formed with a longitudinal seam weld, ie it was made from a flat piece of steel that was rolled into a cylindrical shape and secured with a length-wise weld. Further, the pipeline segment in question was not a single length of pipe, but rather was made up of several short sections, or "pups", welded together. This fact was also not recorded in the GIS. In addition to these basic factual errors, the California Public Utilities Commission (CPUC) and the NTSB have raised numerous other specific examples where the data used for assessing threats, and hence the risk posed by segment 180 of line 132, was incorrect, or when assumptions were made, they were substantially non-conservative.[13] This includes an incorrect depth of cover and an incorrectly high value for the strength of the steel, among other things. So the data used in assessing risk was, in several key areas, just plain wrong.

Engineering records dating from the time of construction in 1956 are incomplete, so perhaps it is not surprising that some of the details had been lost. It is likely that those who originally entered the data were making their best guess (however inaccurate that turned out to be), but there is one further point of interest about the accuracy of the assumed physical property data. The line in question has a diameter of 30 inches and piping of this size was not, and still is not, made without a longitudinal welded seam. If anyone with the right expertise had reviewed the data, it is likely that this basic error would have been identified. Instead, the pipeline was described in the database as "seamless". So it was that the seam weld disappeared without trace, while remaining effectively a ticking time bomb.

Details of organisational relationships and work practices in 1956 when the line was installed are lost in the mists of time, but this faulty weld is a classic latent error. The exact circumstances will never be known, but several people must have been involved in the welding error itself, the quality control and quality assurance practices that failed to detect it, and the decision not to test the line before putting it into service. It seems highly unlikely that this was the result of the action of one individual. Latent errors such as this can sit undetected for decades until other more immediate changes in system operation test the functionality of flawed components. Older equipment can be particularly susceptible to this problem when condition records are not available. The challenge for an organisation that operates such equipment is to find these problems in the operating system before they become part of the causal chain for a serious accident.

This faulty weld and the resulting disaster may at first seem to be the classic "black swan".[14] The metaphor of the black swan is sometimes used in risk management to describe an event which is not expected and has an extreme impact. Most importantly, the concept of a black swan is that such an event could not be predicted based on current understanding. In this case, information was available but not taken into account by those with the power to make decisions. We will talk more about black swans and how to prevent them in Chapter 7.

Chapter

5

Enbridge: deciding whether to repair

It is one thing to inspect part of a pipeline network and identify some anomalies. It is another thing entirely to interpret those results and decide whether further investigation, or indeed repair, is required. In contrast to the San Bruno case, the Marshall pipeline had been inspected on several occasions prior to failure, and significant cracking had been discovered. Yet Enbridge decided not to excavate the pipeline to investigate these problems further; rather, the company relied on ILI results to understand the extent of the corrosion damage to the pipeline, and, on this basis, it was decided not to repair the cracks. These decisions were made, not on the basis of risk; they were based on ritualistic compliance with the relevant legislation.

More generally, complex high-pressure process plant and equipment commonly continues to run despite known minor faults. Companies are regularly faced with decisions regarding what to do in this situation. The most significant issues will require an immediate shutdown for further investigation and repair. Less serious faults may involve some kind of work-around or temporary fix, with a more permanent repair waiting until the next planned maintenance shutdown. Some faults may simply become part of the normal way that the plant operates — the process plant equivalent of the squeaky door or the dripping tap that we never get around to fixing. Given that such decisions are so common, it is useful to review in some detail why Enbridge got this decision wrong at Marshall.

Line 6B was known to have an external corrosion problem and so was subject to what Enbridge called "crack management".[15] The 51.6-inch-long crack that ultimately failed was identified in 2005, but other tests on this line were conducted in 1994, 1999/2000, 2004, 2005, 2007 and 2009. The line was known to be degraded and this was managed by frequent testing rather than repair. Further, all testing was done using ILI. The line was never physically excavated for the cracks to be inspected, and all engineering analysis regarding the need for repair was therefore based on the interpretation of ILI data. The decision as to whether the line needed to be excavated for physical examination and possible repair (at significant cost and production disruption) was based on compliance with detailed prescriptive requirements contained in the regulations.

Of critical significance was the requirement that, for a corrosion-related defect such as this, lines must be excavated if the estimated failure pressure is less than the pressure that would subject any part of the pipeline to the specified maximum yield stress, in this case, 867 psig. For apparently no reason other than the differing interpretations by Enbridge of the regulatory requirements, cracks due to corrosion were treated differently to cracks from other causes. The requirement for generic crack defects was excavation if the estimated failure pressure is less than the hydrotest pressure, that is, in the case of the failed line, 796 psig. The NTSB has criticised Enbridge's choice of the less onerous criteria for a range of technical reasons.[16] It appears that the relevant regulations are somewhat open to interpretation and, yet again, we see that engineering effort has focused on doing the minimum work required to achieve compliance, rather than managing risks to pipeline integrity.

Further, when calculating the failure pressure of the pipeline in its cracked state, Enbridge chose several optimistic values for input data. One particular case to illustrate this is the approach taken to pipeline wall thickness. The 2005 ILI results include measurements of wall thickness which showed that, at the measured location, the pipeline was thicker than the nominal manufacturer's value (although still within the allowable manufacturing tolerance). Despite being a point measurement, this higher value was used for all calculations for this section of pipeline, effectively assuming that the line was stronger than had been specified along its entire length. In fact, the area around the crack (where wall thickness was not measured) had a lower average wall thickness due to the external corrosion that also caused the cracking. In this way, the 2005 assessment treated corrosion and cracking separately, but these cracks were in an area where the wall thickness had been reduced by corrosion, so the wall thickness overall was overestimated and the effective depth of the crack was underestimated. Similarly optimistic interpretations were made of inspection tool tolerance, algorithms for the interpretation of inspection results, and the interaction of corrosion and cracking. These factors led to an optimistic estimate of the failure pressure, ie a finding that the line was stronger than it actually proved to be. This figure was then compared to the hydrotest pressure and the conclusion was drawn that the line did not require repair.

The NTSB has found that a change in any one of the assumptions regarding tool tolerance, wall thickness or the interaction of corrosion and cracking would have resulted in an engineering assessment that the failure pressure was less than the hydrotest pressure and so, by Enbridge's own criteria, the line would have been listed for excavation. Instead, it remained in service for a further five years after the flaws were identified, until it failed in 2010. Similarly, if the criteria used to trigger excavation had been the same for cracks as they were for corrosion, then, even with the various non-conservative assumptions to calculate the failure pressure, the line would have triggered requirements for further physical investigation.

Clearly, using strict compliance as an approach to integrity management without considering risk did not work for line 6B. Enbridge had been using this approach for several years and experienced a similar failure on another pipeline in 2007. In this case, too, calculations of the failure pressure were done based on estimates of the defect size found from ILI. Again, the calculated failure pressure was greater than the hydrotest pressure of the line, and yet it failed the year after the assessment was made. We have no information as to how Enbridge engineers explained this outcome, but whatever lessons were gleaned from this event, the same approach to the assessment of ILI results and the need to repair identified defects continued.[17] The organisation clearly failed to learn from this earlier incident that the method being used to assess the potential for the failure of lines with known cracks was not adequate.

In summary, Enbridge's approach to repairing identified flaws in the pipeline network was based on compliance, with no direct consideration given either to the consequences or the likelihood of a failure. Having adopted an engineering approach based on strict compliance, consistently optimistic assumptions were adopted that resulted in an outcome that no further work was required. It is surely naïve to believe that the assumptions were not adjusted in order to obtain the desired outcome. It seems that Enbridge technical staff put their professional and creative energy into interpreting and managing compliance issues, rather than assessing risk and managing the network, with catastrophic consequences.

Conclusion

We have seen that the PG&E integrity management system was completely inadequate. Integrity management should be about fault identification and repair. Instead, the PG&E system focused on a convoluted series of disconnected, error-prone steps that had no chance of ensuring that the integrity of the pipeline network was maintained over the medium term.

In summary, shortcomings in the system include:

- the system produced only a prioritised list of segments based on threats to integrity. While such a system could, in theory at least, be used to determine where funds should be spent to improve integrity, it makes no attempt to comment on the overall risk acceptability and the total budget required. If the aim of the management system is to ensure that the physical system is safe, then capacity to pay cannot be a primary consideration when planning inspection activities. This is a fundamental problem with management processes based on continuous improvement, and we will have much more to say about this in Chapter 9;

- algorithms for establishing inspection priorities were flawed, both in concept and in execution. Scores obtained for individual threats were combined in a way that resulted in an arbitrary risk index that masked problem areas;

- regardless of the identified threat, higher-risk segments were mostly subjected to direct assessment inspections which can pinpoint pipeline integrity problems for corrosion threats only. This method was chosen because it was cheap, not because it was effective; and

- the physical data that was used to generate the risk information was wrong in many places, some of which would have been obvious if any suitably experienced person had reviewed it.

While this summary highlights many flaws, it must be acknowledged that the integrity management of large pipeline networks is a complex and uncertain business. It requires awareness of the potential for high-consequence but low-frequency events and how such events are best avoided. In the next chapter, we turn to some of the reasons why a focus on long-term public safety is so hard to develop and maintain. Organisations that manage hazardous technology rely critically on the professionalism of their staff. This means maintaining a degree of independence and autonomous decision-making. This goes hand-in-hand with an attitude to work founded on technical and professional curiosity, rather than unquestioning deference to management priorities. The ability to step back and evaluate actions based on professional ethics and public interest, rather than simply following the short-term interests of employers, is a valuable professional quality and one that is necessary to achieve the best safety outcomes.

Instead of representing reality, the risk assessment model generated at PG&E had effectively taken over as reality, as far as decision-making was concerned. Good risk assessment provides those making decisions about risk controls with useful inputs about priorities and effectiveness. To achieve this, the results must be linked to the actual performance of the system — in this case, the history of leaks. As we shall see in Chapter 7, this link was not made at PG&E. Having such a link in place helps to identify and eliminate blind spots and biases, which is also related to the professional curiosity mentioned above.

Bad risk assessment can become a "black box", hiding a lack of rigour behind apparently simple answers. One of the key messages that we would like readers to take away is that the use of risk assessment does not imply that results must always be rolled up into a single all-encompassing index. In many cases, the simplifying assumptions made to produce such an index overwhelm the granularity of the actual factors driving risk. In PG&E's case, combining low-risk and high-risk scores for the same segment into a single index effectively masked problems rather than highlighting them, making the result worse than meaningless when determining what action to take to improve safety.

The Enbridge integrity management system was also problematic in similar ways. In this case, flaws in the line that ultimately failed were identified five years beforehand, but engineering analysis seemed to be focused on developing an argument to show that no repair was necessary. This is based on an attitude of strict compliance with the relevant standard, rather than a consideration of risk — that is, the possible consequences and the increased likelihood of failure, given the identified defects.

Endnotes

1   NTSB Accident Docket DCA10MP008, Document 218, *Public Hearing Transcript — March 1, 2011 (Day One)*, p 152, line 10ff. Available at http://dms.ntsb.gov/pubdms/search/document.cfm?docID=344892&docketID=49896&mkey=77250.

2   NTSB Accident Docket DCA10MP007, Document 239, *IMP Attachment V - Reference-1, IR 376:PDF_2004 HCA Management Plan_Published July 2005, pp 11–18, 20–24, 160–65, 169, 172–81, 188–208, 218–20, 239–41*, p 21 of 57. Available at http://dms.ntsb.gov/pubdms/search/document.cfm?docID=372306&docketID=49814&mkey=76766.

3   Hopkins, A, *Failure to learn: the BP Texas City Refinery disaster*, CCH Australia Limited, Sydney, 2008.

4   Hopkins, A, *Disastrous decisions: the human and organisational causes of the Gulf of Mexico blowout*, CCH Australia Limited, Sydney, 2012.

5   Hayes, J, "Operator competence and capacity — lessons from the Montara blowout", *Safety Science* 2012, 50: 563–574.

6   PG&E's integrity management model included more than 20,000 segments of transmission pipeline. See NTSB Accident Docket DCA10MP008, Document 201, *Interview of Director of Integrity Management*, p 39. Available at http://dms.ntsb.gov/pubdms/search/document.cfm?docID=339974&docketID=49896&mkey=77250.

7   Muhlbauer, WK, *Pipeline risk management manual: ideas, techniques and resources*, Gulf Professional Publishing, Burlington, Massachusetts, 2004.

8   PG&E, *Procedure for risk management RMP-01* (downloaded from the CPUC website). Available at www.cpuc.ca.gov/PUC/sanbrunoreport.htm.

9   NTSB, *Pacific Gas and Electric Company natural gas transmission pipeline rupture and fire, San Bruno, CA, September 9, 2010*, pipeline accident report, Washington DC, 2011, section 1.13.1.

10   Another method of testing is use of DCVG or direct current voltage gradient. There are references to this technique in evidence by some PG&E witnesses, but not in the NTSB report. Since this method tests for external coating integrity and hence the potential for external corrosion, rather than testing integrity directly, it is not canvassed in detail here.

11   NTSB, *Pacific Gas and Electric Company natural gas transmission pipeline rupture and fire, San Bruno, CA, September 9, 2010*, pipeline accident report, Washington DC, 2011, section 2.6.2.2.

12   A version of this story is told in Klein, GA, *Streetlights and shadows: searching for the keys to adaptive decision making*, MIT Press, Cambridge, Massachusetts, 2009, p xiii.

13   CPUC, *Incident investigation report, September 9, 2010 PG&E pipeline rupture in San Bruno, California* (released 12 January 2012), CPUC, Consumer Protection & Safety Division, San Francisco, 2012, section V.

      NTSB, *Pacific Gas and Electric Company natural gas transmission pipeline rupture and fire, San Bruno, CA, September 9, 2010*, pipeline accident report, Washington DC, 2011, section 2.6.

14   Taleb, NN, *The black swan*, Penguin, London, 2010.

15   NTSB, *Enbridge Incorporated hazardous liquid pipeline rupture and release, Marshall, Michigan, July 25, 2010*, pipeline accident report, Washington DC, 2012, p 87.

16   NTSB, ibid, section 2.4.1.

17   NTSB, ibid, p 90.

CHAPTER 6

THE MEANING OF SAFETY

Few people come to work deliberately intending to do a poor job, especially those working in a hazardous industry, such as high-pressure gas pipelines. Nevertheless, as shown in previous chapters, there are many ways in which work done at both PG&E and Enbridge did not achieve the desired outcomes and, in fact, contributed to catastrophe. Despite significant shortcomings, both PG&E and Enbridge were organisations that thought they were focused on safety. In this chapter, we highlight the overall attitude to safety that prevailed in these organisations and the resultant gaps.

At both PG&E and Enbridge, many people in various occupations failed to link their actions to the potential consequences for public safety. This resulted in an accumulation of what Reason calls "latent errors"[1] — faults in the risk defences that had been present for an extended period of time and came to light only when those defences were called on to operate. An apparent lack of problems can be very misleading when taken as feedback that the system is functioning well.

Both organisations had a strong focus on worker safety. Many accident investigations and safety theorists have highlighted the fact that the management of process safety or system integrity issues is not the same as the management of workplace health and safety problems, such as slips, trips and falls, and yet PG&E in particular failed to understand this distinction. It is important to note here that we do not mean to trivialise occupational health and safety. Managing this effectively is also essential to ensure that workers go home safely every day and are not killed or injured by working in confined spaces, repeatedly using poorly designed equipment that causes musculoskeletal problems, or driving poorly maintained work vehicles. Our point is that a focus on these traditional workplace health and safety issues is not sufficient to ensure that workers and the public are not impacted by hazardous facilities such as pipelines.

This lack of understanding appears to have been a factor in the compliance-based approach adopted in both organisations towards process safety issues. When the only question asked is "does it comply?", rather than "is it safe?", it is only a matter of time before an accident occurs.

The last issue addressed in this chapter relates to who has decision-making power in organisations. While senior management always has ultimate control, many organisations rely (knowingly or otherwise) on other professional groups to maintain an excellent safety performance record. When it comes to excellence in safety decision-making, professional groups (such as pilots and doctors) who maintain some degree of independence provide an important counterpoint to management decisions. While such a view is also present in some engineering-based organisations, this perspective seems to have been missing at PG&E and Enbridge.

These four issues are discussed in turn below.

Latent errors and the absence of feedback

We have seen how the actions of individuals at PG&E in widely differing roles contributed to the rupture of the two pipelines and the damage that resulted. Engineers responsible for integrity management planning, maintenance people in the field and control room operators all failed to link their actions to the potential for disaster. Examples include:

- the people who planned the electrical system work at Milpitas Terminal completed work clearance documentation that was not fit for purpose. It provided little detail and did not acknowledge the potential impact of what they were doing, ie the potential to disable key safety systems and cause the overpressure of downstream pipelines;
- the control room operators signed the clearance paperwork despite missing details, not seeking to verify the impact of the planned work on the operational equipment;
- others who were sent copies of the poorly completed work clearance paperwork chose not to intervene;
- the site safety briefings held at Milpitas Terminal on the day of the rupture (in accordance with work clearance procedures) focused only on workplace health and safety issues, not the public safety impacts of the tasks at hand;
- the control room operators had some indications that the pipelines downstream of the Milpitas Terminal were in very real danger of being over-pressured for almost one hour prior to the rupture of line 132, and yet they took no action to isolate the downstream system to prevent this;
- engineers and managers responsible for the integrity management system failed to understand that incorrect and/or missing data in the geographic information system (GIS) influenced the scope of inspection work undertaken and hence had a direct impact on pipeline integrity; and
- engineers and managers put in place an inspection program using an inspection method that was cheap, but did not address the full range of possible threats to pipeline integrity.

Similarly at Enbridge, many practices indicated a lack of understanding of the potential consequences of the actions of individuals, including:

- the operator at the Edmonton Control Centre who shut down line 6B and triggered the rupture of the weakened line failed to interpret numerous alarms as an indication that the line had failed;

- the material balance analyst on duty at the time of the rupture interpreted alarms as a sign of "column separation" rather than pipeline rupture;

- shift B operators, the shift lead and the material balance analyst similarly misinterpreted the alarms that resulted from their attempts to restart flow through the pipeline;

- the control centre supervisor considered the possibility that the line was leaking but dismissed this option on the basis of advice from the material balance analyst;

- engineers and managers responsible for acting on the results of inspection chose not to repair the known cracks;

- those responsible for the pipeline cathodic protection system had not established clear minimum performance standards; and

- it was accepted at Enbridge that the type of coating used on much of the network (including the section that failed) was no longer functional and no additional barriers to pipeline leakage were put in place.*

Chapter

6

It is as if many individuals were unaware of the role they should play in preventing serious accidents and so failed to link their day-to-day actions with the potential for disaster. When seeking to prevent accidents more generally, it is therefore informative to consider why this attitude was so widespread. One possible explanation lies in the way in which adults learn. Much of our learning comes from our own experiences — what we do each day and the outcomes that apparently result. We then generalise life lessons from those experiences. This process of learning can be dangerous when set alongside highly redundant engineering systems.

No organisation that operates a system with the potential for disaster would accept a design where a single failure or error could lead to catastrophe. This applies in engineering, where backup equipment and systems are provided because design engineers know that equipment sometimes fails. They allow for this in their design of automated systems to ensure that overall system performance meets an acceptable standard. This is the science of reliability engineering, and no reliability engineer would confuse the absence of overall system failure with the reliability of any individual component in a complex network.

---

* The last two examples on this list are discussed in detail later in this chapter.

Similarly, organisations usually intend that engineering and procedural risk controls to prevent accidents combine to form layers of protection — that there is redundancy in the system — even if this intent sometimes falls down in practice. This approach is ubiquitous because we know that, despite our best efforts, risk controls are not 100% reliable. The Swiss cheese model is the iconic representation of the idea that accidents happen when weaknesses in systems accumulate so that all controls fail — with catastrophic consequences. The organisational intent is therefore that no single poor decision or inappropriate action has the potential to cause a major disaster if the rest of the system defences are working.

The problem that this creates in trial and error learning about the impact of our own actions should be clear. If individuals are waiting for feedback about the consequences of their actions, they will not receive it until the last defence fails and catastrophe results. Even then, it is possible for some individuals to deny responsibility on the basis that theirs was not the last defence that failed and so, in their mind, their actions are not linked to the accident in any immediate way. Ignoring the potential consequences of one's actions was apparently, at PG&E and Enbridge, "the way we do things around here".[2] With an entrenched norm such as this, any organisation becomes simply an accident waiting to happen when the last barrier fails.

High reliability researchers in the 1990s were the first to shine a spotlight on a special class of organisations that fundamentally cannot rely on trial and error learning because of the severe consequences that may result. Their studies of high-performing organisations emphasise the extent to which such organisations focus on identifying and learning from small failures, faults and errors.[3]

This research has been taken up in many organisations in the form of systems for hazard reporting (also known as incident reporting, near-miss reporting or even operational experience feedback).[4] With such a system in place, all personnel are encouraged to report hazardous events or situations so that appropriate action can be taken to correct each individual case, but also, most critically, so that the stories of small failures are collected and recorded. This data can provide an important source of information for organisational learning, although the temptation for organisations to punish those who self-report errors can destroy trust and quickly remove any reporting incentive.[5] A well-managed scheme with a focus on learning can provide a source of information for those conducting fieldwork of any kind by providing ready access to past problems experienced when undertaking similar activities. Ready access to historical data is also useful for planning engineering work so that taking past problems into account becomes less reliant on individual memory.

We will discuss learning from feedback in relation to integrity management in more detail in Chapter 7, but the general point is made here — that in both organisations the cultural norm was to ignore the consequences of one's actions when it comes to public safety. In the short term, this can seem to be a reasonable thing to do. In contrast, in an effective safety culture, individuals understand their role in major accident prevention. Such a system can withstand occasional errors, but at PG&E and Enbridge, there was a consistency to the attitudes and choices made that contributed to the inevitability of a serious accident.

Protecting both workers and the public

Another way in which PG&E[6] failed to focus its energy on public safety was to limit its perspective on safety to be about workers alone. Focusing on worker safety and measures of worker safety, such as injury rates, masks the potential for low-frequency but potentially high-consequence events. Such events may have more impact on the public than on workers, especially for infrastructure such as pipelines where those people exposed to the consequences of a leak are more likely to be members of the public than workers. Causes are more diverse, more situated at an organisational rather than a workplace level, and so require different strategies to prevent their occurrence.

Chapter
6

This distinction is often described as worker safety versus process safety. This is because the second area has been the focus of much attention in the process industries (chemicals manufacturing, oil refining, and so on). Since many of the substances used in that sector are flammable and/or toxic, there is a substantial incentive to ensure that all fluids are contained under all circumstances. This includes preventing rare but major failures that may have consequences beyond the site boundary into areas where public access is not restricted, as well as smaller spills and leaks that may, for example, occur during maintenance and cause an immediate safety issue for the crew working on the system. Another term that is sometimes used for process safety is "major accident safety". This is a more general term, covering not only the process industries, but also industries such as mining, where roof collapse can cause multiple fatalities, and the airline industry, in which an aircraft crash can kill hundreds. The distinction between worker safety and process safety is perhaps most obvious when the workers are not often physically located near the facilities that can cause an accident, such as is the case with the pipeline industry. In both the accidents of interest here, members of the public were physically impacted by a serious leak, whereas the workers were many miles from the leak location. Since the term "process safety" is potentially misleading in this situation, we have chosen to instead call low-frequency, high-consequence accidents an issue of public safety.

A clear-cut example of where public safety should have been considered, but was not, was in the workplace risk assessment that was done prior to the work at Milpitas Terminal. As described in Chapter 2, this risk assessment considered only the safety of the workers themselves and not the impact that their activities could have on the overall network and hence the safety of the public. Of course, planning for public safety requires consideration long before field crews are about to start work, but this workplace risk assessment represents one last lost opportunity in the case of the San Bruno incident. We can see PG&E's overall corporate attitude to safety matters prior to San Bruno in the letter to shareholders that forms the introduction to the PG&E annual report from 2009:[7]

> "Nowhere has [the pay-off for our intensive efforts] been more true than on our number one priority, safety. In 2009, the three basic safety indicators we monitor all continued to move decisively in the right direction. Thanks to improved training, improved work procedures, and an emphasis on accountability, we achieved major reductions in recordable injuries, lost workdays, and motor vehicle incidents. We exceeded our goals in all three categories. Most extraordinarily, since 2006, we have bettered performance in each of these areas by more than 50 percent. However, notwithstanding these achievements, our safety results are not yet where they must be. On-the-job tragedies took the lives of two workers last year, and our overall safety scores still trail those of the top performers in the industry. Our pledge is that reducing safety incidents will remain a top priority until we reach the absolute goal of zero injuries."

The authors of these words seem to believe that zero injuries to workers is the ultimate safety goal and that their three chosen safety indicators (numbers of recordable injuries, lost workdays and motor vehicle incidents) provide a realistic assessment of the company's safety performance.* Any effort by senior management to focus on safety is admirable in one sense but, of course, by these measures, the San Bruno disaster was not a safety incident. The distinction between worker safety (which is typically dominated by incidents that cause an injury to one person — the so called slips, trips and falls) and public safety is an important one. Public safety is about ensuring that systems are in place to prevent those types of failures that only occur rarely but, when they do, have catastrophic consequences. The distinction is important because the methods used to prevent these two types of events are significantly different.

---

* Perhaps the surest sign that the number of injuries is not a comprehensive goal in its own right, even for worker safety, is the way in which this paragraph treats the deaths of two workers. While this is acknowledged to be a "tragedy", presumably these deaths account for only two injuries and so are not as significant as the overall statistical trend of injury reduction that PG&E has chosen to highlight. We find this paragraph particularly offensive for this reason.

Returning to the subject of trial and error as discussed above, organisations can judge if their strategies for preventing slips, trips and falls are working by relying on trial and error as a performance improvement strategy — that is, using measures such as recordable accidents to judge whether changes to current work practices need to be made in order to improve outcomes. This is analogous to automatic feedback control used in process plants and manufacturing. The desired outcome is specified and the actual outcome for a specific set of inputs is measured. Any deviation from the desired outcome is corrected by making changes to the system inputs.

High reliability organisations (HROs) operate in an environment that requires a different strategy.[8] Accidents must be prevented before they occur in all cases; specifically, no deviation from the required outcome is acceptable. In the language of process control, what is required is feed-forward control. In this type of control scheme, measurements of the system are made and used to predict the future performance of the key parameter. If the predicted performance is not as desired, changes are made to ensure that deviations are corrected before they impact on the overall result. The challenge for HROs is to understand the relationship between the current organisational performance and their future safety performance — what factors need to be measured, recorded or observed, and how they should be changed in order to meet the overall safety performance target. This requires a new suite of safety measures that are not measures of output, such as accident and injury rates.

The failure to distinguish between personal safety and the potential for major accidents is unfortunately common. PG&E focused on worker safety, but did not treat public safety in the same way. PG&E's 2008 annual report includes similar words to those quoted above from the 2009 report. Despite similarly glowing words about the progress made, during 2008, a member of the public was killed and five other people were injured when a leaking PG&E gas distribution line led to an explosion in a house at Ranchero Cordoba, California. PG&E technicians had been on site for four hours at the time of the explosion and one of the technicians was injured in the blast. PG&E was subsequently fined $US38m as a result of this event, although neither the event itself, nor the possible liability, are mentioned in the annual report.[9]

Many organisations fall into this trap (of failing to distinguish between personal safety and the potential for major accidents), but a well-known example is BP in relation to its drilling activity in the Gulf of Mexico before the *Deepwater Horizon* blowout.[10] In one sense, those responsible for work on the *Deepwater Horizon* were very safety conscious. The managers on the rig at the time of the blowout were there partly to present an award to the crew for a creditable seven years' operation without a lost-time injury. Based on this measure of safety, the rig was a stand-out performer within Transocean and BP. More broadly, BP overall claimed a serious commitment to safety, and before the accident reported that "since 1999, injury rates and spoils have reduced by 75%".[11] Hopkins' analysis of the causes of the *Deepwater Horizon* blowout shows that BP had an admirable focus on personal hazards, but an entirely inadequate appreciation of process hazards.

Of course, an understanding that safety includes the public is not on its own sufficient to ensure that high performance is achieved. The Enbridge annual report from 2009 states:[12]

> "Superior service, safety and reliability are integral to Enbridge's customer value proposition. As always, cost management initiatives are balanced with the safe and reliable operation of the Company's system and the need to ensure ongoing customer satisfaction … With respect to safety, Enbridge strives to employ the best available practices and technologies for integrity management, systems maintenance and operations in order to mitigate risks to the public, our employees and the environment."

While this is one of few references to safety in the annual report for that year, it clearly shows some awareness of the broader context of safety decision-making and the link to system integrity. The question is whether this stated commitment was put into practice. In response to two incidents in 2007 and 2008 that caused the deaths of three workers, Enbridge created a new position of Director of Safety Culture. An appointment was made to this new role in May 2010, only two months before the Marshall failure. The person appointed was an engineer by training and was given no special training in safety culture. While reporting at a senior level (to the Senior Vice President, Operations), this person had no staff. The reason for this was because Enbridge "felt that [this was] the best way to really make sure that … safety was owned by everyone, not just a department or an individual".[13] This role also had no allocated budget for making any operational changes, only for conducting training using consultants.

When giving evidence to the National Transportation Safety Board (NTSB) following the accident, the incumbent had some difficulty in articulating what his role is. As he explained, "it was certainly one of those roles where you step into it and you want to try to put a solid equation to it or something that has an equal sign in the middle of it". He went on to explain that this had not been possible in this case; rather, that safety culture was about behaviours. With this in mind, he focused his efforts entirely on field safety activities.[14] Office-based work such as integrity management and senior management decision-making received little attention, and the safety management system that was introduced again focused on field activity only. While this was not clearly articulated, the focus of the safety culture program appears to have been worker safety, not public safety. Clearly, Enbridge also had a lot to learn about the need for organisational focus on public safety issues.

Safety as compliance

Compliance has an almost hallowed status in engineering circles. Compliance with codes and standards, or compliance with regulations (which often refer to those same codes and standards), is seen as the answer to the design of safe facilities and their ongoing engineering management. We agree that compliance is important, but in the apparent absence of a real understanding of the potential for disaster, PG&E's strategy for managing public safety was based simply on compliance with codes and standards — and this was insufficient to ensure safety outcomes. This is the basic approach taken for both maximum allowable operating pressure (MAOP) determination (as discussed in Chapter 3) and the design of the entire integrity management program (as discussed in Chapter 5).

We have already seen that the calculation of the MAOP of PG&E's line 132 was determined based entirely on a view of compliance with the code, including the clauses that permit the grandfathering of testing requirements for old pipelines. The question "is it safe?" is never asked directly, only "does it comply?". This led to an abrogation of responsibility for the safe operation of the system as engineering efforts focused on compliance with regulations. Those regulations had remained weak on the issue of requirements for old pipelines as a result of lobbying by various interest groups over a period of close to half a century.

With regard to integrity management at PG&E more broadly, the overarching company procedure states, "The Integrity Management Program (IMP) is a program established by PG&E to address the integrity management rules in 49 CFR Part 192 Subpart O".[15] This is an important point: the stated purpose of the entire system was not minimisation of the potential for accidents, reduction of risk to an acceptable level or any other goal directly related to safety, but one of compliance with the regulation.[12] The NTSB's Investigator in Chief pointed out during the hearings into the rupture that "the PHMSA regulation or the CPUC's regulations are minimum safety standards. Is there a PG&E policy … that says wherever possible for public safety, thou shalt exceed those standards?". In response, PG&E's Senior Vice President, Engineering and Operations said, "there's not a standard that specifies thou shalt exceed, although there are cases where we do … it's really an engineering judgment".[16] While it may be true that standards were sometimes exceeded in particular cases at PG&E, the overall approach to safety matters was one of compliance.

In Chapter 5, we discussed in detail Enbridge's decisions regarding the repair of line 6B. This is another case in which compliance led to poor safety choices. Looking at the situation more broadly highlights another compliance problem at Enbridge. The monitoring of corrosion cracks and predicting crack growth should have been only one layer in the range of controls that would be expected to be in place to prevent leaks due to external corrosion for a pipeline such as this. The primary risk control would normally be seen as the pipeline coating system. In the case of line 6B, the coating was known to be in a poor state of repair, with significant areas of disbondment, ie places where the coating has come away from the pipeline itself. A second way of controlling external corrosion is the use of cathodic protection (CP), an engineering system that, in this case, relies on a small impressed electrical current to prevent metal loss due to external corrosion in places where the coating may be damaged. The caveat is that CP may not protect against corrosion where the coating has come away from the pipeline but is still intact. In this case, the plastic coating itself may prevent the flow of electrical current, rendering the CP useless to prevent corrosion that may occur if water or other corrosive substances accumulate between the coating and the pipeline.[17] When giving evidence to the NTSB hearing, an Enbridge corrosion engineer was asked what benefit the work of the group responsible for the CP system was expected to have given the major problem with disbonded coating. His reply was, "my only guess would be ... to maintain compliance with regulations and standards".[18] This is surely a staggering suggestion — that an organisation would invest significant time and resources in a system that was known to be effectively useless in order to comply with a standard.

The assertion that the CP system was there for primarily compliance reasons is supported by the way in which the responsibility for the system was organised and how the success of the work was described. Cathodic protection was the responsibility of the operational part of the organisation. A successful CP system was seen by several interviewees as one that operates with a minimum potential of –850 mV, in line with the relevant legislation and standard.[19] Monitoring and measurement of actual corrosion in the field are the responsibility of a different part of the organisation, and the links between the two parts of the organisation prior to the accident were weak at best. Data on actual corrosion rates seems to have been seen as not particularly relevant to those who organise and operate the CP system. This makes sense only if their role was seen as complying with the regulations related to CP, rather than actively preventing pipeline corrosion.

This situation is a clear illustration of the crazy outcomes that can result if the primary strategy for safety becomes simply one of compliance. Cathodic protection is a standard industry method for corrosion control, but writing it into legislation makes it a firm requirement, even in the situation such as existed in parts of the Enbridge system where it was not effective. The temptation then is to assume that CP is effective, even in areas where it is not. Organisations generally do not have a desire to spend money on things that have no practical purpose, and yet operating a CP system on parts of a pipeline network with a substantial disbondment problem is just that — a system that serves no purpose other than meeting a regulatory requirement.

All three examples demonstrate the potential for poor decision-making when compliance becomes a goal in its own right, instead of a means to an end. They also show the danger of a lack of professional, technical curiosity on the part of engineering personnel — a lack of application of fundamental engineering principles to the questions they are attempting to resolve. In the case of the MAOP determination, apparently no one understood the engineering implications of the lack of any safety factor or the potential safety implications of determining the MAOP in this manner. The engineers apparently based their confidence in the system on the fact that it complied with the relevant code. PG&E's engineering work on the integrity management system can be seen in the same terms. Similarly, the technical limitations of Enbridge's CP system were apparently not well understood by those responsible. While it was likely to have been effective in corrosion protection in some areas, it was not effective in disbonded sections. As we have seen, the system was managed as if the primary goal was compliance, rather than corrosion prevention.

Standards and codes are often fundamentally bureaucratic requirements that do not necessarily reflect the reality of the physical world, only the world as their authors collectively see it. In contrast, as one senior pipeline industry figure used to remark, engineered systems obey the laws of nature, not the laws of man.* Engineers forget that to their peril, and to ours.

We shall have more to say about compliance in Chapter 10.

Chapter

6

Professional expertise and responsibility for public safety

Another significant downside of a compliance-based approach to safety is that it writes out of the picture the roles of engineering judgment and professional expertise that are also critical to achieving great safety performance. Other research[20] has shown the extent to which major hazard industries rely on the sense of professionalism of key staff and their identification as members of a professional group. This sits alongside their view of themselves as company employees. One function of such a view of working life is to foster an awareness of the public trust held by professionals in hazardous industries and the sense of responsibility for one's actions that goes with that. The only data available on which to assess whether such a social network was in action at PG&E is from the various transcripts of interviews and hearings. Statements made by PG&E technical staff in these forums are driven by their response to questioning so they are somewhat constrained, and yet there is little sense from them that they feel a sense of professional responsibility for the results of their actions. Responses are almost without exception framed by

---

* This saying is widely attributed in the Australian pipeline industry to Ken Bilston, former chair of the Committee responsible for AS 2885, the Australian pipeline standard.

reference to company systems, rather than reference to any broader understanding of responsibilities or context.

As with many modern organisations, PG&E and Enbridge are highly bureaucratised. What we mean by this is that management is the dominant profession and that the most senior managers, ie those at the top of the organisational hierarchy, set the goals of the organisation and the methods by which those goals will be achieved. Top managers are very powerful and the role of other members of the organisation is simply to implement strategies that are determined at the top — essentially, to follow instructions.

For organisations that operate hazardous technologies and have a high level of safety performance, this is only a partial view of the way power is distributed. In organisations such as airlines, offshore oil and gas production and nuclear power generation, professional groups other than managers also have significant power and authority when it comes to safety decision-making. Think of an airline pilot in the cockpit. A professional who holds this role operates within company systems, but also holds the ultimate decision-making authority for the safety of the aircraft. Doctors are responsible for the safety of their patients, independent of the hospital that may employ them. Offshore oil and gas platforms, chemical plants and nuclear power stations all operate in a somewhat similar manner. There is always one individual present at the facility who has the ultimate authority for in-the-moment decision-making. When things start to go wrong, that individual decides whether operations can continue or must be shut down. This power-sharing applies also to key engineering decisions, not just operational decisions that must be taken under time pressure. Major decisions made regarding the design of new facilities or the engineering analysis of the state of existing plant and equipment all rely on professionals, as well as managers.[21] The high reliability researchers were the first to highlight this arrangement, calling it "deference to expertise", noting that, in high reliability organisations, top managers sometimes defer to others who are more qualified to make specific critical decisions.

To ensure that the best choices are made, it is not enough for authority to be simply delegated down the organisation. A key facet in this arrangement is a sense of identity linked to an expert's profession (not just their employer) which encourages decision-makers to think independently. Members of a profession are often characterised by qualities such as a sense of public trust, an ability to act independently of their employer, valuing technical expertise, and adherence to a code of professional ethics.[22] It is these attitudes that provide a huge benefit to organisations, as such individuals provide an additional valuable perspective on what makes the system safe, rather than simply acting in line with management priorities at all times, irrespective of the specific circumstances.

This discussion is not meant to portray technical professionals as "white knights" and managers as "black knights". The interaction between these different professionals is more subtle than that. Finding the right balance between conflicting organisational goals — costs, schedule, safety — is difficult only because these are *all* legitimate concerns. Organisations can cope with some degree of cost overrun or production loss, and so, to some extent, these issues can be managed by trial and error, but when it comes to public safety, the challenge is to get the decision right every time. This requires the imagination to see what might go wrong and the foresight to see how it might be avoided without becoming so conservative that nothing is achieved.

The *Challenger* space shuttle disaster is a vivid example of what can happen when this capacity is lost to decision-makers. The explanation for this accident centres on the decision made to launch the shuttle, despite evidence of technical problems with the solid rocket booster seals. Vaughan's analysis[23] challenges simple explanations of managers acting as "amoral calculators" overriding the concerns of the engineers. Instead, she focuses on the way in which almost all those involved were sucked into the momentum of the preparations for launch, such that the burden of proof was reversed from its usual orientation. Instead of a launch only taking place if all involved were convinced that there was no unacceptable risk, engineers were put into a position of being asked to prove that their concerns about seal damage on previous missions meant that this launch was unsafe. This significant structural change in the way the decision to launch was made effectively silenced the independent voice and removed those engineers who had concerns from the decision-making process. A diversity of views was effectively eliminated.

Most of the people interviewed by the NTSB as part of the investigations into the San Bruno and Marshall accidents seem to see themselves as company employees first and members of a profession (such as engineering) a poor second. Actions are taken in line with company procedures or regulatory requirements, not because a particular course of action is the "right" thing to do. This is in stark contrast to our work with professionals in other organisations (including in the pipeline sector[24]), where key technical staff have a sense of vocation towards their work. At best, this is valued by their employers and their actions and/or advice on safety matters are trusted by senior managers, even when there may be significant cost implications.[25]

Research has also shown that experts learn by sharing stories of past mishaps — not only serious incidents, but also near misses that reinforce professional values and norms.[26] This seems to have been significantly absent at PG&E, where leaks were repaired and then almost deliberately forgotten. As mentioned in Chapter 7, a significant problem with line 132 occurred in 1988. It is perhaps worth noting that the manager with direct responsibility for the integrity management program at the time of the rupture joined PG&E in 2004, straight from university. There appears to be no reasonable way in which she could have known of the 1988 incident, since stories about past leaks were not "kept alive" within the company.

Without a strong sense of professional expertise, the decision-making approach adopted at both PG&E and Enbridge was completely reliant on the requirements set by the organisation. As we have seen, this simply means compliance with the regulations.

Conclusion

At both PG&E and Enbridge, technical personnel went about their everyday activities apparently largely unaware of the impact that their actions were having on the long-term safety of the public. This state of affairs continued at PG&E because, when the organisation spoke about safety, attention was fixed on workers, rather than the public. At Enbridge, safety was understood (at least by those who wrote the highest-level documents) to include both workers and the public, but this apparently had little impact at a working level. This attitude can prevail because of the level of redundancy in managing complex technologies. Accidents are rare and so we can be lulled into a false sense of security by lack of feedback — until something goes wrong in a catastrophic way.

In both organisations, the primary strategy for ensuring public safety was the management of system integrity by means of compliance with regulations. The key question in people's minds was "does it comply?", rather than "is it safe?". Removing safety from direct consideration in this way allows effort to be diverted into minimising effort, so as to conform to the letter of the law, rather than taking a common sense approach based on the potential for harm and basic engineering principles. It also de-emphasises the role of professional staff and their moral responsibility for public safety that originates from professional, rather than company, values.

We will say much more about compliance as a safety strategy in Chapter 10.

Endnotes

1   Reason, J, *Managing the risks of organizational accidents*, Ashgate, Aldershot, 1997.

2   See Ed Schein's famous definition of organisational culture in Schein, E, *Organisational culture and leadership*, Jossey-Bass, San Francisco, 1992.

3   Weick, KE and Sutcliffe, KM, *Managing the unexpected: assuring high performance in an age of complexity*, Jossey-Bass, San Francisco, 2001.

Weick, KE, Sutcliffe, KM and Obstfeld, D, "Organizing for high reliability: processes of collective mindfulness", in Sutton, RI and Staw, BM (eds), *Research in organizational behavior*, JAI Press Inc, Stamford, 1999.

4   Hayes, J, "Incident reporting: a nuclear industry case study", in Hopkins, A (ed), *Learning from high reliability organisations*, CCH Australia Limited, Sydney, 2009.

5   Hopkins, A, "Identifying and responding to warnings", in Hopkins, A (ed), *Learning from high reliability organisations*, CCH Australia Limited, Sydney, 2009.

6   Again, we have more data available about PG&E's attitude than Enbridge and so, for this reason, this section focuses primarily on PG&E.

7   PG&E, annual report, 2009.

8   Weick, KE and Sutcliffe, KM, *Managing the unexpected: assuring high performance in an age of complexity*, Jossey-Bass, San Francisco, 2001.

     Weick, KE, Sutcliffe, KM and Obstfeld, D, "Organizing for high reliability: processes of collective mindfulness", in Sutton, RI and Staw, BM (eds), *Research in organizational behavior*, JAI Press Inc, Stamford, 1999.

9   CPUC, *Incident investigation report, September 9, 2010 PG&E pipeline rupture in San Bruno, California* (released 12 January 2012), CPUC, Consumer Protection & Safety Division, San Francisco, 2012, p 151.

10   Hopkins, A, *Disastrous decisions: the human and organisational causes of the Gulf of Mexico blowout*, CCH Australia Limited, Sydney, 2012.

11   National Commission on the BP Deepwater Horizon Oil Spill and Offshore Drilling, *Deepwater: the Gulf oil disaster and the future of offshore drilling, report to the President*, 2011, p 218.

12   Enbridge Inc, *2009 annual report: where energy meets people*, 2009, p 38.

13   NTSB Accident Docket DCA10MP007, Document 324, *Interview of McEachern-Director of Safety Culture-11-14-11*, p 9. Available at http://dms.ntsb.gov/pubdms/search/document.cfm?docID=369651&docketID=49814&mkey=76766.

14   NTSB Accident Docket DCA10MP007, Document 324, ibid, p 22.

15   PG&E, *Procedure for risk management RMP-01* (downloaded from the CPUC website). Available at www.cpuc.ca.gov/PUC/sanbrunoreport.htm.

16   NTSB Accident Docket DCA10MP008, Document 218, *Public Hearing Transcript - March 1, 2011 (Day One)*, p 132, line 25ff. Available at http://dms.ntsb.gov/pubdms/search/document.cfm?docID=344892&docketID=49896&mkey=77250.

17   Worse still, in some circumstances, CP can actually accelerate corrosion under disbanded coating, but the NTSB ruled out this mechanism as contributing to the failure of line 6B.

18   NTSB Accident Docket DCA10MP007, Document 348, *Interview of Sporns-Supervisor of Corrosion Program Group-12-06-11*, p 35. Available at http://dms.ntsb.gov/pubdms/search/document.cfm?docID=369740&docketID=49814&mkey=76766.

19   NTSB Accident Docket DCA10MP007, Document 348, ibid, p 113.

     NTSB Accident Docket DCA10MP007, Document 308, *Interview of Harris-Corrosion Control Coordinator-12-06-11*, p 14. Available at http://dms.ntsb.gov/pubdms/search/document.cfm?docID=369585&docketID=49814&mkey=76766.

     NTSB Accident Docket DCA10MP007, Document 287, *Interview of DeWitt-Cathodic Specialist-07-29-10*, p 6. Available at http://dms.ntsb.gov/pubdms/search/document.cfm?docID=369495&docketID=49814&mkey=76766.

20   Hayes, J, *Operational decision-making in high-hazard organizations: drawing a line in the sand*, Ashgate, Farnham, 2013.

     Hayes, J, "The role of professionals in managing technological hazards: the Montara blowout", in Lockie, S, Sonnenfeld, DA and Fisher, DR (eds), *Routledge international handbook of social and environmental change*, Routledge, London, 2013.

Chapter
6

21   Hayes, J, "Cost, schedule and public safety: design team dynamics and the impact on safety decision making", APIA, EPRG and PRCI 19th Biennial Joint Technical Meeting, Sydney, 2013.

22   Middlehurst, R and Kennie, T, "Leading professionals: towards new concepts of professionalism", in Broadbent, J, Dietrich, M and Roberts, J (eds), *The end of the professions? The restructuring of professional work*, Routledge, London, 1997.

23   Vaughan, D, *The Challenger launch decision: risky technology, culture and deviance at NASA*, University of Chicago Press, Chicago, 1996.

24   Maslen, S, "Organisational factors for learning in the Australian gas pipeline industry", *Journal of Risk Research* 2014, DOI: 10.1080/13669877.2014.919514.

25   Hayes, J, *Operational decision-making in high-hazard organizations: drawing a line in the sand*, Ashgate, Farnham, 2013, chs 6 and 9.

26   Hayes, J and Maslen, S, "Knowing stories that matter: learning for effective safety decision-making", *Journal of Risk Research*, 2014, DOI: 10.1080/13669877.2014.910690.

CHAPTER 7

DEALING WITH UNCERTAINTY

Managing the potential for major hazard accidents is difficult because such accidents are rare — even given the problems with the San Bruno pipeline, it operated for more than 50 years before it failed. This long lead time highlights the level of conservatism and redundancy in entrenched industry practices. Sometimes equipment can operate without incident for years, even with serious underlying faults. The pipeline ruptures dramatically highlight how difficult it is to be sure that a system is safe, because track record is not a reliable predictor of future success. Maintaining an organisational focus on the potential for disaster in the face of little feedback is a challenge faced by other industries such as nuclear power generation, offshore oil and gas exploration and production, aviation, and similar. Put simply, we learn most readily by experience, by trial and error, but this is not a strategy that is effective for preventing rare events, that is, it is not acceptable to wait for a major failure to learn that the integrity management system is not functioning as intended.

Ensuring the integrity of networks of high-pressure buried pipelines is a complex and uncertain undertaking, especially when the assets are decades old. Engineering records are likely to be incomplete, and direct evidence of the physical state of the equipment will be available for only a few selected locations. As we have seen in Chapter 5, both PG&E and Enbridge relied on risk assessment to determine where to focus their attention. More broadly, integrity management can be seen as an exercise in planning — deciding what tasks need to be completed in what sequence and the implications of the results for further activity. Thinking about the best way to go about planning under conditions of significant uncertainty can give us further clues as to why things went so wrong and how these traps can be avoided. Again, this chapter draws heavily on decision-making at PG&E, given that there is more public domain information available.

Planning is a straightforward instrumental activity (a means to an end) in cases where uncertainty is low. Integrity management is a very different case. As a system for recording and managing information, the geographic information system (GIS), plus the associated procedures for integrity management algorithms, constitute a form of planning. For complex pipeline networks such as those operated by PG&E and Enbridge, many things are not certain. Not all lines have been tested or inspected, so their condition can only be inferred. Data about old pipelines may be missing. More than that, sometimes engineering data itself may be unreliable in ways that are not obvious, so there are "known unknowns" and "unknown unknowns". Effective planning to achieve an important goal such as network integrity is much more difficult under these conditions, and planning itself becomes a critical activity. When uncertainty is high, planning can become a symbolic, rather than an instrumental, undertaking and it appears that this was the case at PG&E. When planning takes on a primarily symbolic role, the purpose of the plan becomes "asserting to others that the uncontrolled can be controlled".[1] In this situation, symbolic plans represent a fantasy — in the sense of a promise that will never be fulfilled — and are often couched in special vocabulary which then shapes discussion. The danger is that the plan takes on a life of its own and organisational effort is focused on managing the plan, rather than taking care of the physical system itself.

The significant uncertainty surrounding integrity management also raises the question of whether events such as San Bruno and Marshall are predictable at all. The concept of the black swan is relevant here.[2] This metaphor has been gaining currency in risk and safety discussions about the predictability of improbable but damaging events. A black swan is an event which is not expected and has an extreme impact. Most importantly, the concept of a black swan is that such an event could not be predicted based on available knowledge. Seeing accidents as black swans potentially introduces a fatalistic view of accident causation, or at least a sense of not being responsible. On the other hand, it is important to note the situated nature of the definition — it's about limitations to current knowledge held by a specific individual or group. It does not seem to be pushing the metaphor too far to point out that black swans are in the eye of the beholder. For the Noongar people of southern Western Australia, black swans were, and still are, common. The metaphor therefore highlights the critical role of knowledge and learning, specifically a diversity of views, experience and expertise, in planning and risk management.

Fantasy planning

The idea of fantasy planning in the face of significant uncertainty explains both how and why the integrity management system at PG&E had taken on a symbolic rather than a functional role, and therefore how other organisations might avoid this trap.

As described in Chapter 5, the integrity of PG&E's pipeline network was assessed using a complex qualitative model. The original aim of the model was to represent current reality (the physical pipeline network) in such a way as to allow future problems (ie leaks) to be predicted and hence prevented. We have already seen how flawed the implementation of this concept was and yet PG&E saw this system in much more glowing terms. As the Director of Integrity Management explained to an NTSB hearing:[3]

> "[We] calculate the risk of all our segments ... there's 20,000 transmission segments [in the GIS] ... Using that analogue equation, we put number values on them. They're risk values, they're not probabilistic. It's more about this pipe looks worse than this other pipe, which looks better than the other pipe but not as bad as the first pipe type of concept. We can provide a ... general graph of how many segments we had in which level of risk priority ... what it looked like in 2001 and what it looks like in 2009, after a series of mitigation ... all the mitigation we perform on it through DA and ILI. We drive that down through a program we call Risk Management Top 100. That's an annual capital investment in some portion of the top 100 highest risk pipelines ... You are effectively driving the risk to zero."

An example of the graphs to which he refers is reproduced in Figure 7.1. It appears to show the number of pipeline segments on the vertical axis plotted against risk index on the horizontal axis, indicating that most segments have a low score. This gives a clear picture of where integrity management efforts should be directed — to the tail of the curve on the right-hand side and those few segments that have a high-risk index score.

On further consideration, the description given by this manager seems oddly disconnected from the actual performance of the pipeline network. The stated goal is not to reduce actual leaks (leak data is not referred to), but to drive down on paper, as seen in Chapter 5, the output of a demonstrably flawed risk assessment process.

Chapter

7

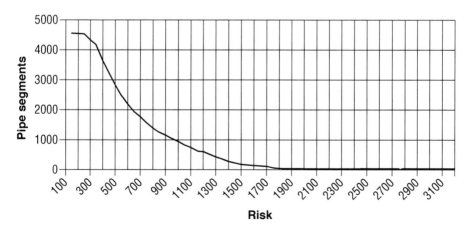

FIGURE 7.1: Pipeline risk profile[4]

So what was PG&E's attitude to leaks? In an interview with the National Transportation Safety Board (NTSB), the Director of Integrity Management was also asked about PG&E's leak history and, in particular, the identified causes of leaks and the actions taken to prevent further leaks. His repeated response was "there's leaks and there's repairs".[5] He and other PG&E staff members interviewed by the NTSB have great difficulty understanding why the organisation should have done anything as a result of leaks other than repair each one. This "fix and forget" attitude was further revealed during the formal investigation when, eight months after the accident, PG&E advised the NTSB that, in 1988, there had been a longitudinal seam failure on a section of line 132 approximately nine miles from the 2010 rupture location. This leak and other earlier problems with seam defects were not taken into account in integrity management planning because "PG&E stated that when it transitioned to its GIS in the late 1990s, only open (that is, unresolved) leak information was transferred. Closed leak information — such as the October 27, 1988, leak, which had been repaired — was not transferred to the GIS".[6] Trend analysis or formal feedback to the planning of integrity management or modelling of system integrity does not seem to have been understood as critical activities to ensure that the integrity management system was effective at predicting and preventing problems.

In an attempt to explain why the 1988 leak was not relevant to ongoing integrity management or to the San Bruno rupture in particular, PG&E highlighted that this was only a small leak and had no structural integrity implications. However, the California Public Utilities Commission (CPUC) has laid out in its evidence an internal PG&E memo from 1989 that highlighted the discovery of significant quality problems with the welds dating back to manufacturing, and the likelihood that the leak was related to these weld problems.[7] It seems likely that integrity engineers understood the significance of the identified manufacturing problem when they wrote this memo in 1989, although this information was not taken forward into ongoing integrity management planning. In total, 11 leaks or seam defects on the line that ultimately failed were recorded over the period 1948 to 2011.[8] These failures were repaired and then dismissed from the collective memory. No broader implications of these failures were considered and, as a result, valuable opportunities for learning in this uncertain environment were not taken up.

Research into "high reliability organisations" (HROs) has shown that "fix and forget" is the antithesis of the attitude in companies with the best safety performance.[9] HROs are preoccupied with failure and see every small problem as a chance to learn more about their facilities and so prevent major disasters from occurring. A pipeline company that was aspiring to be an HRO would be at pains to remember past small leaks, not to forget them, and to draw as much information as possible from the data by way of technical and organisational lessons about the circumstances of the leaks and what they might individually and collectively reveal. In contrast, at PG&E, the effectiveness of the integrity management model was not checked or "benchmarked" (to use common industry jargon) in any way against the actual record of leaks from the system.[10]

Another way in which the model itself was disconnected from reality was the input data used. We have already highlighted the problem with data about the failed segment, that is, the longitudinal seam weld that failed did not exist in the integrity management system because the line was recorded as seamless. The NTSB found many similar errors in the data that was used as the basis for risk assessment. Engineering records for old equipment can be sketchy to say the least, and PG&E had a significant problem with lack of basic data about the system. Nevertheless, the NTSB found that "many of the pipe segments for which records had missing, assumed, or erroneous data had previously been exposed in connection with [external corrosion direct assessment (ECDA)] excavations as part of the integrity management program".[11] In other words, corrections could have been made to some erroneous GIS data as a result of feedback from the inspection program, but this was not done.

In a similar vein, PG&E's procedure for integrity management planning talks about how the data on which decisions are based will be sourced. As the procedure says, "for the risk analysis process, the Company has chosen attributes based upon available, verifiable information or information that can be obtained in a timely manner".[12] This is an astonishing statement, apparently saying that the company will use data that it has to hand or it will use anything else that it can come up with quickly. In contrast to this, after the rupture, PG&E's Senior Vice President, Engineering and Operations, stated that "there is a method for dealing with lack of information, and again it's a conservative value that's placed in. I think what then needs to be done … is that we would need to have, based on the criticality of the attribute or aspect or data field that was missing, some set of steps taken to determine physically in the field … what the real case is".[13] In fact, there were fields in the database that were blank seven years after this system of integrity management was established and, as discussed earlier, the data entered in the system for line 132 was not conservative.

Chapter

7

This substantial disconnect between the field engineering and the office-based modelling appears also to have led to major logical inconsistencies in the way inspection work was planned. As described earlier, by 2004, parts of line 132 had been inspected for external corrosion. No problems were identified and the line was then reassessed as low risk. Available information on the importance of an identified serious materials defect and other data about the leak history of the line were not used in the risk assessments that set inspection priorities. Further, as discussed in Chapter 5, PG&E's inspections on this line were all performed using ECDA (ie dig up a section of the line and check for local problems), a procedure that is not capable of identifying seam weld problems. In summary, despite evidence of materials problems, inspections focused on another possible leak cause (external corrosion) and evidence of materials issues was systematically ignored.

What engineers supposedly knew about the system overall had come to be grounded in elaborate algorithms and graphs that purported to show that risk was declining, and yet this analysis was not validated and so was only tenuously linked to the actual level of danger. The model was a fantasy and did not adequately represent the real network at all. This is not to suggest that, in circumstances like this, companies or individuals are deliberately fabricating models or plans in order to deceive themselves or others. The impact of fantasy documents is more subtle than that. In the face of significant uncertainty, earnest attempts to plan can lose touch with reality because this gives us the psychological certainty that we crave when put into an uncertain situation. In such situations, we lack control over outcomes and this is a powerful stress producer for individuals and for companies.

Leaders can do much to address this by focusing their attention on the right things. If managers focus on graphs and direct their staff to drive the risk down, you can be sure this will happen, whether or not this is actually having an impact on the real level of danger posed by the system. Again, this is not to suggest that staff will behave dishonestly, but they will focus on efforts to refine algorithms to show notional improvements, address high-risk contributors only rather than checking for flawed data that may be misrepresenting lower-risk results, and have little interest in verification of the model results against real-world outcomes if success is based on something else entirely — a graph which shows risk to be declining.

A key factor in maintaining this flawed view about the integrity of the network appears to lie in the extent to which the integrity management system was isolated from information about the actual state of the pipelines in the ground. Leaders would do better to focus on actual leak results, in addition to model outcomes, as a measure of success. As highlighted earlier, PG&E's integrity management system was not linked to its leak history. If such a link had been in place, it is likely that questions would have been raised about the accuracy of the model and hence its usefulness in preventing further leaks.

In the face of uncertainty around the integrity of the complex network, PG&E adopted an optimistic view of the state of the buried pipelines based on the outputs of their risk modelling and integrity management planning. Evidence was available that the model was flawed and that the system might not be as safe as the model suggested, but all such evidence was ignored. Instead, ongoing management decisions were based on the model, rather than the reality. The model had become an end in itself, rather than a means to an end — a way of providing an illusion of control, rather than a way of preventing accidents.

Relying on flawed models such as this is an example of the organisational problem identified by Turner and Pidgeon as "disaster incubation", that is, where organisational beliefs about the control of hazards are at odds with actual events.[14] As the name suggests, this lack of real control around accident prevention makes disaster more likely. This should not be new news. As well as Turner's work dating originally from 1978, high reliability researchers have been encouraging us for several decades to look for the lessons contained in small failures, rather than wait for a major disaster to tell us that our risk control efforts are not effective.

Apparently, there are some who still have yet to hear this message.

Black swans

Signs of possible danger can be hard to pin down, especially when planning exercises generate graphs and other data that appear to be evidence that all is well. An alternative to the unfounded optimism brought about by fantasy planning is to take a fatalistic view — a view that rare events are impossible to predict in advance and so cannot reasonably be prevented. This equally problematic perspective has been fostered by the black swan metaphor which we have increasingly been hearing as an excuse for the failure to prevent serious accidents. The argument runs along the lines that "we've been doing our best to predict and prevent such events, but what can you expect when they are black swans?". This metaphorical shrug of the shoulders in the face of major accidents is what Paté-Cornell calls the "stuff happens" view of risk analysis.[15]

In fact, such a view is not a fair interpretation of the black swan idea as put forward by Taleb.[2] While his work focuses significantly on the financial markets, he draws extensively on examples from other domains — although few, if any, that are directly related to industrial safety. Nevertheless, there are some key warnings in his work that provide food for thought in our efforts to prevent disaster. First, he is at pains to point out that a black swan is not an objective phenomenon; rather, that black swans are the result of a lack of knowledge by those with the power to make decisions — be that individuals or a group. The knowledge needed to prevent disaster is likely to exist somewhere in the system, but a black swan event can occur when decision-makers are unaware and so do not intervene. To use an extreme example, it is not accurate to say that no one knew about the Twin Towers attack on September 11, 2001. Those who were planning to carry out these terrorist attacks knew that they would occur, but those responsible for United States security did not. In the industrial safety context, remembering that black swans are subjective phenomena encourages us to consider who else might know something that could be useful in preventing disaster and to seek out these alternative voices.

Another warning drawn from Taleb's work is the danger of over-reliance on risk models. Models such as these rely on past experience to predict future performance. In the pipeline context, the output of an integrity management model is a prioritised list of segments for inspection. It is very difficult to validate this information, ie to determine whether it accurately identifies those segments that are most likely to be lower integrity.

The risk index model system uses algorithms as described in Chapter 5. Other risk models use concepts such as fault trees and event trees to enable experience of smaller failures to be extrapolated to address the potential for less likely but more serious events. The risk index model assesses each segment against a predetermined list of possible failure causes, ie threats. As such, any risk model is only considering the worst scenarios that the risk analyst was able to imagine. To say this another way, a scenario has to be seen as credible before it is included in a risk assessment. Such models do not have the power to predict completely new scenarios, as even the best models are heavily reliant on knowledge of history to both build the model and benchmark the results.

This means that, even using the best model, there is no guarantee that all black swans will be prevented. The clear problem here is that the past is not a completely reliable predictor of the future for rare but serious events. Or to use a more trivial example, from the perspective of a turkey, life looks pretty good based on historical data right up until the week before Thanksgiving. Our challenge then becomes how to find those cases that the model fails to take into account.[16]

Taleb's work gives several clues about strategies that are applicable to major accident prevention. The first is to look beyond models and seek a diversity of views about what could go wrong and what the most vulnerable parts of the system are. Going back to the Thanksgiving example, don't just ask the turkeys. But if we are not to rely solely on engineering models for integrity management planning purposes, how else can we decide what to inspect? One answer is to consider a diversity of views on where serious problems are mostly likely to occur. What do other organisations with similar problems do? What do other sectors do? How is this issue managed in other parts of the world? Where do the operations or maintenance personnel perceive the biggest problems to be? The global pipeline industry accident record includes accidents, many of which have been investigated by the NTSB and other agencies, with detailed causal information released into the public domain. This could have been used by PG&E to undertake targeted reviews of its system to see if the company was vulnerable to the problems identified elsewhere. There are many diverse sources of knowledge available that organisations rarely take advantage of because doing so is time-consuming.

In a similar vein, Taleb says that, when seeking to avoid black swans, we should "avoid optimisation and learn to love redundancy".[17] In organisations that operate complex systems, it is considered normal to have redundancy in key engineering systems — two pumps instead of one, backup power supplies, and so on. On the other hand, most communications and processes involving people have been optimised dramatically in recent years. Duplication is seen as inefficient and redundancy is seen as wasteful, rather than a valid strategy for improving system reliability. As a senior gas company executive told us recently, "we don't have time to think. We outsource thinking". If this attitude is prevalent, is it any wonder that rare events prove to be beyond the capacity of many organisations to prevent in the medium term?

We note in passing that Taleb's strategies for minimising the potential for black swans have much in common with the findings of high reliability researchers. Researchers in this field[18] have also highlighted the value of learning from small failures, seeking a diversity of views, being sensitive to operations, committing to resilience, valuing reliability over efficiency, and other similar qualities. Taleb does not reference this work, but no doubt he would endorse many of the strategies for avoiding catastrophic events that are proposed by researchers in this field.

Even with the careful treatment of input data, the best possible algorithms, plus the benchmarking of results against available leak data, the results of risk modelling are not validated in any rigorous sense. Knowledge is dangerous if we don't understand the limitations of its applicability, so one additional way to improve model validation would be to spend part of the inspection budget inspecting segments that the model had NOT chosen as high priority. In most situations, the greatest uncertainty in risk estimates is around frequency (rather than consequence), so another form of insurance would be to spend a small proportion of the overall budget (say 10%) on testing systems that modelling has shown to be high consequence but low risk due to an estimated low frequency of failure.

The events at San Bruno and Marshall may be black swans in the sense that Taleb originally intended, but this cannot be used as an excuse as to why these and similar incidents are unavoidable. The message from black swan theory is that models, however robust and well-tested, are not to be trusted implicitly. A better outcome will always be obtained if more diversity is taken into account when collecting data for decision-making.

Conclusion

Planning under conditions of uncertainty is difficult. A wise organisation manages to achieve a balance between rosy-hued optimism that all is under control and

Chapter

7

fatalism that accidents are beyond its control, but this takes a great deal of effort and focus from leaders.

Beware of presentations of risk, especially those that show that risk is declining and everything is under control. Always ask how such data has been verified against actual field experience.

Constantly look for ways to challenge models. For example, consider spending part of the field budget on inspections driven by consequence, rather than by risk.

Endnotes

1   Clarke, L, *Mission improbable: using fantasy documents to tame disaster*, University of Chicago Press, Chicago, 1999, p 16.

2   Taleb, NN, *The black swan*, Penguin, London, 2010.

3   NTSB Accident Docket DCA10MP008, Document 201, *Interview of Director of Integrity Management*, pp 39–40. Available at http://dms.ntsb.gov/pubdms/search/document.cfm?docID =339974&docketID=49896&mkey=77250.

4   From PG&E, *Procedure for Risk Management RMP-01*, p 12 (downloaded from the CPUC website). Available at www.cpuc.ca.gov/PUC/sanbrunoreport.htm.

5   NTSB Accident Docket DCA10MP008, Document 201, *Interview of Director of Integrity Management*, p 36, line 22ff. Available at http://dms.ntsb.gov/pubdms/search/document.cfm?do cID=339974&docketID=49896&mkey=77250.

6   NTSB, *Pacific Gas and Electric Company natural gas transmission pipeline rupture and fire, San Bruno, CA, September 9, 2010*, pipeline accident report, Washington DC, 2011, pp 109–110.

7   CPUC, *Rebuttal testimony of Raffy Stepanian*, CPUC, Consumer Protection & Safety Division, San Francisco, 20 August 2012, p 24, line 16ff. Available at ftp://ftp.cpuc.ca.gov/SanBrunoReports/ CPSD%20Reply%20Testimony.pdf.

8   NTSB, *Pacific Gas and Electric Company natural gas transmission pipeline rupture and fire, San Bruno, CA, September 9, 2010*, pipeline accident report, Washington DC, 2011, p 39, Table 2.

9   Weick, KE and Sutcliffe, KM, *Managing the unexpected: assuring high performance in an age of complexity*, Jossey-Bass, San Francisco, 2001.

     Weick, KE, Sutcliffe, KM and Obstfeld, D, "Organizing for high reliability: processes of collective mindfulness", in Sutton, RI and Staw, BM (eds), *Research in organizational behavior*, JAI Press Inc, Stamford, 1999.

10   PG&E had in place a "self-assessment" system which was supposed to check on the overall effectiveness of the inspection program. Primary documents such as audit reports are not in the public domain, but the NTSB described the system as "superficial" and pointed out the very slow follow-up, eg two years, between the December 2007 audit and the internal response.

11   NTSB, *Pacific Gas and Electric Company natural gas transmission pipeline rupture and fire, San Bruno, CA, September 9, 2010*, pipeline accident report, Washington DC, 2011, p 108.

12   PG&E's Procedure RMP-6, p 22, quoted in CPUC, *Incident investigation report, September 9, 2010 PG&E pipeline rupture in San Bruno, California* (released 12 January 2012), CPUC, Consumer Protection & Safety Division, San Francisco, 2012.

13 NTSB Accident Docket DCA10MP008, Document 218, *Public Hearing Transcript - March 1, 2011 (Day One)*, p 184. Available at http://dms.ntsb.gov/pubdms/search/document.cfm?docID =344892&docketID=49896&mkey=77250.

14 Turner, BA and Pidgeon, NF, *Man-made disasters*, Butterworth, Oxford, 1997.

15 Paté-Cornell, E, "On 'black swans' and 'perfect storms': risk analysis and management when statistics are not enough", *Risk Analysis* 2012, 32(11): 1823–1833.

16 Some readers may recognise this story as Bertrand Russell's much-quoted illustration of the fundamental problem with inductive reasoning.

17 Taleb, ibid, p 371.

18 Weick, KE and Sutcliffe, KM, *Managing the unexpected: assuring high performance in an age of complexity*, Jossey-Bass, San Francisco, 2001.

Bourrier, M, "The legacy of the high reliability organization project", *Journal of Contingencies and Crisis Management*, 2011, 19: 9–13.

Chapter

7

CHAPTER 8

SETTING SENIOR MANAGEMENT PRIORITIES

The primary evidence used in this study to analyse the actions of PG&E employees in the lead-up to the San Bruno rupture is mainly testimony from middle managers and field workers, plus company records, procedures and publications that have been made available to the public via the National Transportation Safety Board (NTSB) investigation process. Other aspects are drawn directly from the three official investigation reports as described in Chapter 1. There is little evidence that comes directly from senior management of the company since those individuals were not directly involved in the investigation processes.[1,*] Despite this, senior management views on safety and integrity management pervade our analysis. Models of safety culture and organisational accidents stress the importance of senior management attitudes due to the power that they hold over staff, both directly and indirectly. It is because senior management as a group is so influential that we can draw some tentative conclusions about the attitudes and motivations of the PG&E Board and executive team, and how they contributed to the catastrophic events that unfolded. This chapter focuses on PG&E, but it is likely that senior management at Enbridge suffered from some of the same failings. While these issues are potentially relevant to Enbridge, no data was available on these points in the inquiry material.

It is the role of leaders to direct the attention of the organisation to what is important, and PG&E senior management has demonstrably failed in this. An analysis such as this does not seek to allocate blame to individuals (neither managers nor workers), but rather to seek explanation in order to prevent recurrence. There is little doubt that the PG&E Board and executive thought that they were doing the best for shareholders. It is not difficult to imagine that cutting costs on maintenance and inspection was seen as a question of efficiency — the elimination of needless costs. In the case of PG&E, this situation was exacerbated by the overall corporate structure of the company's activities which put constraints on income and gave the organisation a direct incentive to minimise operating costs, including maintenance and inspection, in order to maximise profit.

The executive remuneration incentive scheme was also aligned with the organisational focus on cost minimisation and profit. The important implication

---

* The exception is the Independent Review of PG&E, where the reviewers did speak directly to senior levels of that organisation. See CPUC, *Report of the independent review panel, San Bruno explosion*, prepared for the CPUC, revised copy, 24 June 2011. Available at www.cpuc.ca.gov/NR/rdonlyres/85E17CDA-7CE2-4D2D-93BA-B95D25CF98B2/0/cpucfinalreportrevised62411.pdf.

here is that, if it was considered at all, senior management may have assumed that, if the cuts went too deep, there would be warning signs in the form of small incidents in time for managers to take action before any major failure occurred.

Trial and error learning such as this is a common, and often effective, strategy for management decision-making but, as we have already noted, this strategy is fraught with danger if applied to the potential for high-consequence but low-frequency accidents. Cost-cutting in this environment requires decision-makers to have (or have unfettered access to) expertise about the integrity of the system, and the impact of decisions to be carefully considered in advance. It appears that this was not the case at PG&E. We have no direct information on Board decision-making processes, but all Board positions at the time of the accident were held by individuals with qualifications in telecommunications, finance and law, rather than those with experience in gas engineering or high-pressure gas transmission operations.[2] This supports the view that relevant experts, if they existed in the organisation, were not in key decision-making roles. Absence of incidents is not absence of risk in this industry, and the executive team apparently failed to understand this.

Expenditure on maintenance and inspection at PG&E

Most organisations that operate hazardous facilities are fundamentally driven by profit. Many are publically listed organisations with statutory responsibilities to shareholders to maximise returns. It is increasingly common in this situation for investigations into major accidents to highlight the cutting of maintenance budgets as a contributing causal factor.[3] But, as we shall show below, the corporate structure of PG&E gave those at the top even more incentive to cut spending in their attempts to increase shareholder returns.

PG&E's overall corporate structure consisted of two separate organisations — an operating company and a holding corporation that was publicly traded. Prior to the rupture, the activities of the operating company provided the main source of revenue for the parent corporation, and the governance arrangements of the two organisations were substantially merged. The corporation was effectively required to manage the safety and profit of the activities conducted by the company in order to manage its own profitability. The other major constraint on the profitability of the company were the restrictions on income. Due to its status as a monopoly gas and electricity supplier within parts of California, PG&E the company is a "regulated entity". While it aims to provide a financial return on investment for its parent company (PG&E Corporation), some key aspects of the financial environment differ from a typical company operating in a competitive market. Given that PG&E has a monopoly on retail energy supply in northern California, customer interests are represented by the California Public Utilities Commission

(CPUC). Each year, PG&E presents to the CPUC a document known as a rate case (which includes a budget showing capital and operating expenditures), in order to justify the rate that it wishes to charge consumers to achieve its mandated target rate of return. In this way, a regulated entity is prevented from making excessive profits by overcharging consumers in a monopoly market. Once a rate case is in place, the only flexibility the company has to increase profitability is to reduce costs (since income is essentially fixed).

Critically, the organisation can also never fail in the way that an entirely profit-driven enterprise can. In 2001, due to problems with the California electricity market, PG&E had been forced to pay very high prices on the spot market, without the ability to pass on the costs to customers. As a result, the company filed for bankruptcy. The government could not allow the company that provides domestic gas and electricity supply to northern California to stop trading, so the CPUC agreed to a settlement which stabilised PG&E's finances and included, among other things, a guaranteed rate of return on equity. On the other hand, the regulatory arrangements permit higher than mandated rates of return. Once the CPUC has approved PG&E's annual budget, there are no further checks that actual expenditure matches that which was estimated. If expenditure does not meet projected levels, there is no commensurate reduction in costs to consumers. This situation simply leads to a higher rate of return and higher profits to the listed parent company.

The CPUC summed up the situation as follows:[4]

> "Unfortunately, PG&E Corporation relies solely on the profit of the regulated entity (PG&E Company) for its financial health. A publicly traded corporation that relies exclusively on growth derived from the profitability of a single regulated utility will, by its very nature, be biased towards shareholder financial interests when weighed against safety."

As part of its investigation into the incident, the CPUC commissioned an audit of expenditure on safety at PG&E.[5] The report found that PG&E consistently spent less on the maintenance of its gas facilities than it was reporting to the CPUC in its submissions regarding costs to consumers. During this period, PG&E's rate of financial return was higher than required, ie the company could have afforded to spend more money on maintenance while still meeting minimum financial criteria. The report also found that PG&E specifically cut costs related to integrity management by deferring projects and changing assessment methods (from in-line inspection to the cheaper, but less effective, method of direct assessment). The auditors found that "integrity management and maintenance project budgets were viewed as discretionary funding that could be reduced to meet the overall budget targets set by executive management" and, further, that "managing a gas system to the brink of regulatory non-compliance and accepting an elevated risk of

Chapter

8

system failures, is not industry practice".[6] As we have already described in Chapter 5, the level of spending necessary to reduce risk in the interests of safety must be based on an assessment of absolute risk. Simply using risk as a way to prioritise an inadequate maintenance budget does not ensure that accidents will be prevented.

This strong focus on cost minimisation is not something that PG&E attempted to hide. The CPUC noted that, in its 2010 mid-year progress report, PG&E directed its employees to:[7]

> "Continue to focus on productivity and efficiency to meet our budget and profitability target. To maximize the value for money we spend to operate, use our precious financial resources as carefully as we would our own personal funds."

Criticism of the physical state of PG&E's facilities was not limited to underground assets. The CPUC also criticised PG&E after the rupture for the condition of the equipment at the Milpitas Terminal, saying, "the evidence listed below proves that in fact Milpitas Terminal was in a deteriorated condition and demonstrates a pattern of PG&E allowing the equipment to remain in service until failure rather than to replace items before the end of their practical lifetimes".[8] In summary, the CPUC's list is as follows:

(1) the equipment was old. The CPUC maintains that it was well into the "wear out" phase of the bathtub curve. Instrumented systems were not fail-safe and the design did not meet current standards;

(2) there were loose wires and poorly made connections because of insufficient space on terminal blocks; and

(3) documentation was poor, including incorrectly labelled circuits, out-of-date drawings, missing labels, and maintenance and operations manuals incorrectly referring to obsolete equipment.

Evidence suggests that PG&E's lack of effective resourcing was widespread and included cuts to maintenance, inspection and engineering analysis to support these activities. This attitude was apparently driven as an across-the-board policy as part of a senior management focus on cost minimisation.

Thinking specifically about the impact on integrity management, as explained in detail in Chapter 5, the PG&E integrity management system used a prioritisation system based on continuous improvement where, in theory, at least the model identified how best to spend the available budget. The problem for safety is that the question "what needs to be done to ensure that the system is safe?" is never asked — only "given our available funds, how best should we spend them?". In an environment where funds are limited, an integrity management system designed like this does not provide any warning that safety is being compromised.

Remuneration structures and bonuses[9]

Remuneration systems, as embodied in the performance agreements of top managers, serve powerfully to focus everyone's attention on key drivers, typically, production targets, cost minimisation and personal safety. If there is nothing in the system of pay to focus attention on the management of the potential for major accidents, then this is likely to be done very poorly, if at all. Reports following the 2005 BP Texas City Refinery disaster also drew attention to this issue. The Baker Panel concluded that "a significant proportion of total compensation of refining line managers and supervisors [should be] contingent on satisfactorily meeting process safety performance goals …".[10] As one observer remarked: "Managers did not act to prevent Texas City because every incentive and potential penalty they faced told them not to."[11]

A similar situation existed at PG&E. Prior to the rupture, PG&E Company and PG&E Corporation held joint Board meetings and the financial status of the corporation was used in incentive schemes for senior personnel in the company. The CPUC report details the size of these incentive arrangements under the long-term incentive plan (LTIP). This program was still in place in an unchanged form in late 2012:[12, 13]

> "In 2006, the 'Chairman, CEO, and President' (one position) received a $7 million LTIP award, equally split between Restricted Stock Units and Performance Shares. If PG&E's shareholder return is in the top rank of its comparative group, that person could receive the full award of up to $10.5 million ($3.5 million Restricted Stock Units and $7 million Performance Shares). The Chief Executive Officer (assume of PG&E Utility) received a $3 million award, also equally split, which could render a full award of up to $4.5 million bonus ($1.5 million in Restricted Stock Units and $3 million in Performance Shares) in 2006."

PG&E's short-term incentive plan (STIP) also apparently lacked a focus on safety. Details do not seem to be in the public domain, but the revised program has been severely criticised by the CPUC.[14] It reports that the plan is made up of 30% financial aspects, 30% customer satisfaction and 40% a composite of seven other goals, of which safety is one. The unfortunate message given by the Board in this situation is that, even following the disaster, it is "business as usual" as corporate drivers are unchanged.

Research suggests that we can expect financial incentives to be motivational in corporate settings in two ways. The first is through the top-down creation of a culture. Within incentive arrangements, there are often group-wide measures that only group leaders can directly influence. Group-level incentives provide group leaders with a personal financial interest in improving performance in relation to metrics included in bonus calculations, such as shareholder return and injury rates. Leaders create culture by what they attend to and what they prioritise, and such cultures percolate down through the organisation.[15] Where the lead from the top is sufficiently insistent, it will end up affecting the culture of the work group, that is, "the way we (the workers) do things around here". This is obvious enough in the case of production pressures, but there is plenty of evidence that, where top leaders use a range of carrot and stick options to inculcate certain safety-relevant behaviours (eg fastening seat belts, wearing hard hats), these behaviours also become part of the culture of the work group. The net effect is that leaders, who may themselves be financially motivated, end up creating cultures that exert influence on lower-level managers and workers, independently of any financial incentives that may be paid.

There is also evidence that financial incentives motivate corporate employees through their connection to personal evaluation against their individual performance agreements. Evaluations are based on the supervisor's judgment about how well the individual has performed in relation to the various tasks specified in the performance agreement. This system of performance evaluation can have powerful effects on people's behaviour. One of the inquiries into the blowout in the Gulf of Mexico found that individual performance agreements often specified that employees should contribute to the cost-reduction goals.[16] The inquiry also found that, of 13 employees whose evaluations it examined, 12 had documented ways in which they had saved the company large sums of money. Clearly, the incentive arrangements were having the intended effect. Presumably, the motivation was, in part, financial. But there is much more to it. The performance evaluation is a judgment by the supervisor of how well the individual is performing. The evaluation involves praise, faint praise, or criticism — powerful psychological incentives are therefore also at work.

That we are motivated by many things does not automatically undermine the strategy of paying financial incentives to corporate employees, because financial incentives do not rely on economic self-interest alone for their effect. Instead they tap into a number of human motives, among them the need for approval, the need to belong and the need to be recognised as making a valuable contribution — all higher-level motives that transcend purely economic considerations.

This leads to the second issue that is vital to address if companies continue to rely on external rewards. The problem is that, wherever a goal is expressed in terms of some numerical measure, this can encourage attempts to manage the measure, independently of the phenomenon or activity being measured. To take a particularly relevant example in the present context, bonuses paid to managers for cost-cutting can result in cuts to maintenance, training and supervisory staff — all factors that have been implicated in major accidents.[17] This is not an unethical response, since those making the cuts do not necessarily appreciate the possible consequences. The increased risk of a major accident is simply an unintended consequence of a cost-focused bonus system.

The same potential for unintended consequences can also be observed with one of the most common measures of injury, the lost-time injury rate. A lost-time injury is an injury that results in time away from work other than the day on which the injury occurred. If people are brought back to work the day after an accident and placed on alternative duties, a potential lost-time injury is no longer a lost-time injury. While return to work can often be justified from an injury management point of view, there is plenty of anecdotal evidence of people being brought back to work purely as a means of managing the measure.[17] Many industries have sought to overcome this particular problem by focusing on broader injury categories, such as all injuries requiring any medical treatment or even first aid. But these, too, are measures that can be manipulated. A bandage or sticking plaster is first aid only if it is administered by a nurse; if it is self-applied, it does not count. There is evidence that companies encourage self-application for this reason.[17]

These cautionary comments about the use of injury rate data are equally applicable to process safety indicators, such as loss of containment events. The United States standard on process safety indicators (API RP 754) defines a Tier 1 event as one that involves a gas release of 500 kg or more per hour, while a Tier 2 event is a gas release of between 50 and 500 kg per hour.[18] However, it is not easy to determine the quantity of gas released. Weight must be calculated from estimates of pressure, size of hole and duration of release. That the figures are estimates only leaves plenty of room for data manipulation. If the estimate comes in at 495 kg, then it is only a Tier 2 event, not a Tier 1, and such a number has almost certainly been adjusted to achieve this outcome.

These outcomes are ubiquitous and bedevil most systems of bonus payments that operate in the private sector. Bonus arrangements need to be carefully designed to guard against these perverse consequences. If companies are not willing and able to give this the attention it deserves, the evidence is that financial bonuses should be abandoned.

In summary, the research indicates that financial incentives are likely to be effective in focusing attention on major accident prevention if they are designed effectively. This was not the case at PG&E, where bonuses are linked to financial performance. It is not difficult to imagine a system where senior management bonuses are linked to integrity management outcomes — although care would need to be taken to ensure that *real* measures of system integrity were developed. A poor system can be counterproductive in that it can encourage individuals to manage the measure and may even divert attention away from key safety issues. For example, we would not wish to see bonuses linked to the modelling results described in Chapter 7, given the lack of connection to the real state of the pipeline network.

Regulated utility companies and public corporations

As described earlier, the merging of the corporate requirements of a regulated entity (PG&E Company) with those of a publicly traded corporation (PG&E Corporation) was apparently the source of many of the senior management attitudes that led to the pipeline rupture. Formerly state-owned utilities (including natural gas supply) have been privatised, or at least corporatised, in many countries. It is also common for these organisations to be subject to economic regulation similar to that in place for PG&E in order to protect customers from excessive pricing as a result of monopoly operations by suppliers. For this reason, the details of how this corporate structure contributed to the events at San Bruno are of broad interest.

As part of the CPUC's investigation into the San Bruno rupture, the agency has summarised (see Table 8.1) what it sees as the major organisational and cultural differences between a regulated entity and a publicly traded corporation.[19] This makes sobering reading when viewed from the perspective of public interest, which depends on both safe pipeline operation and equitable gas prices.

These two types of organisations differ significantly, driven by the ultimate goal of their activities. Corporations have a statutory responsibility to maximise profits, and the primary group whose interests they must consider are shareholders. On the other hand, a regulated entity has service provision as its primary task, so it is required to satisfy the economic regulator which acts on the behalf of customers. These differing goals lead to quite different logic regarding the best interests of the entity when it comes to spending money on long-term safety.

As physical assets age and the risk of failure increases, corporations have several options available to them. They can decide to spend significant funds on inspection and repair to ensure that risk remains at acceptable levels. Alternatively, they may decide to shut down old facilities or sell a risky asset in order to remove the risk to their corporation, especially if repair costs are judged to be too high. There is always a temptation to reduce spending on safety to maximise profits. Corporations provide products and services in a competitive environment, so spending less can offer a market advantage, at least in the short-term, but corporations also have an incentive to avoid disasters due to the financial and reputational damage that would result.

Critically, regulated entities provide a public essential service and so cannot fail. Several years prior to the San Bruno pipeline failure, PG&E experienced severe financial difficulties as a result of fluctuations in the California electricity market. As a result, it was effectively "bailed out" by the state of California. When the senior management of an organisation knows that it has this to fall back on, risk management must surely become a lower priority. This is hardly good news for public safety.

TABLE 8.1: Culture of a regulated utility v culture of a publicly traded corporation[20]

	Regulated utility	Publicly traded competitive corporation
Ultimate goal:	Provide safe and reliable service at just and reasonable rates.	Maximise profits.
Answers to whom:	Needs regulator approval when determining budget, expenditures, retail prices, and capital investments to ensure the provision of safe and reliable service at just and reasonable rates.	Needs shareholder approval (via Board) when determining budget, expenditures, retail prices, and capital investments to maximise profits.
Obligations:	Obligation to serve, therefore, can never fail. In general, utility is a monopoly and customers cannot switch to another provider.	Not obligated to serve. If a customer is not economic, company can choose to not serve or adjust its rates to cover the risk. Customers can switch to another provider and the company can fail.
Revenue determination:	Regulator determines retail rates to ensure rates are just and reasonable and the company can recover its approved cost estimates.	Management proposes and Board approves retail rates to: ensure a stable and/or growing client base which can be lower or competitive with competitors' rates; and enable the company to cover accounting and economic costs.
Recourse in case company cannot generate enough revenue to cover costs:	Ask regulator, and regulator can authorise rate relief to ensure justifiable costs are covered.	Can only squeeze operations expenses to a point where they impact service and customers will switch providers.
How return on equity is generated:	Relies on regulator for rate of return on its costs to serve.	Relies on investments in portfolio to maximise profits, and relies heavily on innovation, advertising, and company image to retain and grow customer base.
If company is run poorly or inefficiently:	Regulator can impose regulations or provide authority to recover only costs necessary to efficiently operate the utility. If additional revenue is needed to ensure efficient and reliable delivery of utility service, regulator can authorise rate relief and provide cost recovery. If necessary, regulator can issue fines, or require remedies.	Customers switch to a competitor and the company is either forced to change or fails.

Chapter

8

cont …

TABLE 8.1: cont

	Regulated utility	Publicly traded competitive corporation
Ethics:	Ensure ratepayers are provided safe and reliable service at just and reasonable costs.	All legal tools can be employed, such as out-advertise, out-market, out-innovate, and differentiate the products to eliminate the company's competition or any entity that gets in the way of maximising profits.

Given this difference in the interests of the two types of organisation, arguably the worst possible option for long-term safety is to have a regulated entity owned by a publicly traded corporation without clear management boundaries between the two. Knowing that the regulated entity can never fail effectively provides the risk management strategy for the corporation. Senior management can then cut maintenance costs, knowing that, if disaster does strike, the organisation will be insulated from the worst financial impacts. The CPUC maintains that this is effectively what happened at PG&E, with the two organisations run as one, merging the two sets of qualities in a way that maximised short-term profits without considering the rights of ratepayers.

Conclusion

Cutting spending on activities that ensure long-term system safety is a strategy that unfortunately many organisations have adopted, to their ultimate cost. PG&E's total fines in relation to San Bruno remain under discussion at this time, but they are likely to total approximately $US2.5b.* This dwarfs the sums of money saved by reduced expenditure on operations and maintenance.**

While this chapter has focused on the situation at PG&E, cost was also a driver in decision-making at Enbridge about the timing of the repair to the cracked pipeline. When asked by the NTSB about how decisions were made about whether to repair or replace the cracked pipeline, one Enbridge manager described engineering analysis work that had been done to determine when the crack was expected to have grown to

---

* PG&E has been indicted by both state and federal agencies. As this book goes to print, PG&E has been fined $US1.4b by the state of California, and incurred $US635m in additional costs for its mandated pipeline modernisation program (see http://docs.cpuc.ca.gov/PublishedDocs/Published/G000/M105/K451/105451860.PDF). Federal fines are yet to be finalised but are estimated at around $US1b.

** Overland Consulting estimates that operations and maintenance budgets were underspent by $US2.8m on average over the 14-year period 1997 to 2010. See Overland Consulting, *Focused audit of Pacific Gas & Electric gas transmission pipeline safety-related expenditures for the period 1996 to 2010*, Leawood, Kansas, 30 December 2011, pp 1–2.

the point that repair criteria were triggered.[21] We have already described in Chapter 5 how optimistic Enbridge's assumptions were in making this assessment. As part of his answer to this question, the manager also described the negotiations that the company had commenced with customers to recover the estimated quarter of a billion dollars replacement cost. It is surely not unreasonable to assume that these two activities were linked so that, at the very least, there would be a strong preference at Enbridge to avoid carrying out the repairs until the cost issue was resolved. Again, by way of comparison, the clean-up cost linked to the spill was over a billion dollars.[22]

The comparisons above of course do not take into account the total cost of such accidents to society and specifically to those directly impacted. Nevertheless, even these simple comparisons show that ignoring the potential impact of major disasters is not in the best interests of shareholders. A well-structured remuneration scheme can act to focus attention on key long-term safety issues, such as activities designed to ensure system integrity, and we have described some of the key design features of such a system.

We don't pretend that these issues are simple or that safety decision-making is straightforward. As we have shown, sometimes even Boards are to some extent hamstrung by industry structural issues that extend beyond the bounds of any individual corporation. Nevertheless, these important governance issues for modern organisations that operate hazardous technology remain under-addressed. Until that situation changes, accidents will continue to occur.

Endnotes

1   The exception is the independent review of PG&E where the reviewers did speak directly to senior levels of that organisation. See CPUC, *Report of the independent review panel, San Bruno explosion*, prepared for the CPUC, revised copy, 24 June 2011. Available at www.cpuc.ca.gov/NR/rdonlyres/85E17CDA-7CE2-4D2D-93BA-B95D25CF98B2/0/cpucfinalreportrevised62411.pdf.

2   See the PG&E 2009 annual report for a list of Board members and the PG&E website for profiles. The CPUC independent review has also made this point (see p 17).

3   See, for example, Hayes, J, "Operator competence and capacity — lessons from the Montara blowout", *Safety Science* 2012, 50: 563–574.

     Hayes, J and Hopkins, A, "Deepwater Horizon — lessons for the pipeline industry", *Journal of Pipeline Engineering* 2012, 11(3): 145–153.

     Hopkins, A, *Failure to learn: the BP Texas City Refinery disaster*, CCH Australia Limited, Sydney, 2008.

     Hopkins, A, *Disastrous decisions: the human and organisational causes of the Gulf of Mexico blowout*, CCH Australia Limited, Sydney, 2012.

4   CPUC, *Rebuttal testimony of Raffy Stepanian*, CPUC, Consumer Protection & Safety Division, San Francisco, 20 August 2012, p 56. Available at ftp://ftp.cpuc.ca.gov/SanBrunoReports/CPSD%20Reply%20Testimony.pdf.

5   Overland Consulting, *Focused audit of Pacific Gas & Electric gas transmission pipeline safety-related expenditures for the period 1996 to 2010*, Leawood, Kansas, 30 December 2011 (for CPUC).

6   Overland Consulting, ibid, pp 1-1, 1-2.

7   CPUC, *Addendum to the CPSD staff report, section IX I.12-01-007*, 2012, p 4. Available at www.cpuc.ca.gov/NR/rdonlyres/3B91847C-5435-42E0-AEFC-92662D3AC5D2/0/AddendumtoCPSDStaffReport.pdf.

8   CPUC, *Rebuttal testimony of Raffy Stepanian*, CPUC, Consumer Protection & Safety Division, San Francisco, 20 August 2012, p 42. Available at ftp://ftp.cpuc.ca.gov/SanBrunoReports/CPSD%20Reply%20Testimony.pdf.

9   This section draws on Hopkins, A, and Maslen, S, *Risky rewards: how company bonuses affect safety*, Ashgate, Aldershot, 2015.

10   Baker, J, et al, *The report of the BP US refineries independent safety review panel*, BP, London, 2007, p 251.

11   Bergin, T, *Spills and spin: the inside story of BP*, Random House, London, 2011, p 85.

12   CPUC, *Rebuttal testimony of Raffy Stepanian*, CPUC, Consumer Protection & Safety Division, San Francisco, 20 August 2012, p 59. Available at ftp://ftp.cpuc.ca.gov/SanBrunoReports/CPSD%20Reply%20Testimony.pdf.

13   CPUC, *Addendum to the CPSD staff report, section IX I.12-01-007*, 2012, p 2. Available at www.cpuc.ca.gov/NR/rdonlyres/3B91847C-5435-42E0-AEFC-92662D3AC5D2/0/AddendumtoCPSDStaffReport.pdf.

14   CPUC, *Rebuttal testimony of Raffy Stepanian*, CPUC, Consumer Protection & Safety Division, San Francisco, 20 August 2012, p 59. Available at ftp://ftp.cpuc.ca.gov/SanBrunoReports/CPSD%20Reply%20Testimony.pdf.

15   Schein, E, *Organisational culture and leadership*, Jossey-Bass, San Francisco, 1992.

16   Transcript of the testimony of The Joint United States Coast Guard/Bureau of Ocean Energy Management Investigation (re *Deepwater Horizon*), PM session, 7 October 2010, p 148.

17   Hopkins, A, *Failure to learn: the BP Texas City Refinery disaster*, CCH Australia Limited, Sydney, 2008.

18   American Petroleum Institute, *Recommended Practice 754, Process safety performance indicators for the refining and petrochemical industries*, 2010.

19   CPUC, *Rebuttal testimony of Raffy Stepanian*, CPUC, Consumer Protection & Safety Division, San Francisco, 20 August 2012, p 59. Available at ftp://ftp.cpuc.ca.gov/SanBrunoReports/CPSD%20Reply%20Testimony.pdf.

20   Based on CPUC, ibid, pp 57–58.

21   NTSB Accident Docket DCA10MP007, Document 308, *Interview of Irving-Director System Integrity and Compliance-12-05-11*, p 13ff. Available at http://dms.ntsb.gov/pubdms/search/document.cfm?docID=369585&docketID=49814&mkey=76766.

22   See http://desmog.ca/2013/08/26/official-price-enbridge-kalamazoo-spill-whopping-1-039-000-000.

CHAPTER 9

EFFECTIVE SAFETY REGULATION

With the benefit of hindsight, the flaws in the integrity management of PG&E's line 132 and Enbridge's line 6B are very clear. In addition to questions regarding the management of this issue within each operating company, this leads directly to questions about the role of the pipeline technical regulator and why such serious shortcomings were apparently not identified or acted on by the regulatory agencies involved. The problems were so significant that it calls into question the whole structure of the regulatory regime in place for pipelines in the United States. For this reason, we start our exploration of this issue with a broad review of safety regulatory practices.

In most jurisdictions, worldwide, prior to the mid-1980s, the safety of workers was regulated through a set of prescriptive rules with which employer organisations were required to comply. In some cases, the rules were contained in the regulations themselves, and in other cases, the regulations referred to established industry-based standards. The primary safety focus was on physical dangers associated directly with the work undertaken — issues such as exposure to toxic chemicals or asbestos, electrocution, and work at height or in a confined space.

In the offshore oil and gas industry, a series of major disasters in the 1970s and 1980s highlighted the limitations of this approach and provided a driver for major regulatory change in Europe and Australia (but not in the US). In 1980, the *Alexander Kielland,* a drilling rig that had been converted to a "flotel" to provide offshore accommodation for almost 400 workers, was operating in the Norwegian sector of the North Sea and 123 people died when the facility sank in heavy weather as a result of a structural failure. This incident graphically highlighted the limitations of a regulatory approach that, at that time, largely ignored low-frequency but potentially high-consequence events.[1]

Several years later, in 1987, the *Piper Alpha* platform in the United Kingdom sector of the North Sea was destroyed by a series of fires and explosions, and 167 people died as a result. The public inquiry that followed[2] recommended major changes to various aspects of the offshore industry, including the philosophy underlying the extant regulatory regime. Operating companies were thus required to prepare and submit a safety case that would be accepted (or not) by the regulatory authorities. A safety case literally requires companies to demonstrate that their facility is sufficiently safe by describing the processes by which hazards are identified, risks are assessed and, most importantly, that they are appropriately and sufficiently controlled in an ongoing manner. The overall requirement is the demonstration that risk has been reduced to a level that is as low as reasonably practicable (ALARP).

The proposal for regulatory change was adopted in the UK and, with only minor amendments, this regulatory regime remains in place today.[3] The *Report of the public inquiry into the Piper Alpha disaster* (often simply called the Cullen Report after its author) was also very influential in policymaking outside the UK. Holland made similar changes to both offshore and onshore petroleum regulation,[4] and Australian regulation of the offshore oil and gas industry also moved to a safety case regime, first for new developments and then for all existing facilities. Australian pipeline regulations have also been modified in all jurisdictions to follow this general approach. This type of regulation is often called *goal-setting*, as opposed to the previous *prescriptive* approach, because the regulations describe processes that must be put in place, rather than specific measures that must be taken to ensure safe operations.[5]

Risk-based regulation of this kind (with or without using the term "safety case") is now widespread in complex socio-technical systems — both in the industrial sector and for public infrastructure. Demonstration of adequate risk management practices is now commonly used in Europe and Australia as the basis for the regulation of worker and public safety in aviation,[6] nuclear power,[7] chemicals[8] and railways,[9] among others. The perceived benefits of this approach include placing the responsibility for safety clearly with the operator (rather than the regulatory body), allowing innovative solutions and the use of innovative technology, and focusing enforcement efforts onto risk controls that are specific to the hazards and risks on each facility.

We start this chapter by expanding on these ideas with a description of the key features of goal-setting regulation. We then move to a discussion of the regulatory regime in place in the US pipeline sector, why this failed to prevent the events at San Bruno, and how goal-setting regulation would be more effective.

In addition to an effective structure, any regulatory regime needs a clearly articulated enforcement philosophy with sufficient experienced regulators to implement it and a range of effective enforcement tools for them to use. These issues are discussed in the third part of this chapter, which concludes with a summary of why "grandfathering" is inconsistent with goal-setting regulation.

Principles of goal-setting regulation

In a goal-setting regulatory regime, as the name suggests, the specific technical requirements are not fixed but, rather, developed as part of the regulatory process. At first glance, this might sound as if it is softer than under a prescriptive regime but, in fact, if implemented well, the opposite is the case. Rather than specifying technical requirements, goal-setting legislation specifies the process that operators must follow to develop an understanding of what risk controls must be in place. The cornerstone of this process is the requirement to demonstrate that risk is as low as reasonably practicable (ALARP). This is so important that it takes the form of a general duty — the overarching requirement that this type of legislation places on operators. Once the process has been followed and the outputs regarding specific risk controls to reduce risk to ALARP are known, then ensuring that those controls remain in place becomes a regulatory requirement. In this way, goal-setting legislation is more targeted, more effective and potentially tougher than the older-style prescriptive requirements. Organisations can be held to account to do what they said they would do.

Although the acronym "ALARP" is commonly used in risk management and engineering, the origins of the concept are in law. There is no simple definition of the legal expression "reasonably practicable", but legal interpretations in the UK and Australia can be traced to the definition by Asquith LJ in *Edwards v National Coal Board* (1949):[10]

> "'Reasonably practicable' is a narrower term than 'physically possible' and seems to me to imply that a computation must be made by the owner, in which the quantum of risk is placed on one scale and the sacrifice involved in the measures necessary for averting the risk (whether in money, time or trouble) is placed in the other; and if it be shown that there is a gross disproportion between them — the risk being insignificant in relation to the sacrifice — the defendants discharge the onus on them."

Regulation based on this principle is often called safety case regulation because the document submitted by the operator to the regulator is often called a safety case — literally the case made by the operator that the facility or activity is safe enough, ie that risk is insignificant compared to the effort required to reduce it further. In order to make such a demonstration, safety cases take a variety of regulated forms, but they are typically required to include a risk assessment component and a management system component. The risk assessment component sets out what is required to reduce risk to ALARP, and the management system component sets out policies and the procedural framework for continuous improvement to ensure that risk remains sufficiently low as operations proceed.

A safety case style risk assessment has four critical components:

(1) It must include rare but serious events — low-frequency, high-consequence risks.

The risk assessment portion of a safety case is focused on process safety or public safety (see Chapter 6), not specifically worker safety (which is typically addressed primarily by the safety management system portion of the safety case). As such, the focus is on the long-term prevention of catastrophic events. Given the complex and facility-specific causal chains that these types of events have, this component of the safety case gives regulatory oversight of such events in a way that is difficult under prescriptive regulation.

(2) All relevant stakeholders must be involved in the preparation of the risk assessment and must understand their subsequent role in accident prevention.

The focus of the safety case for an operating facility is how things are actually working in practice. Even in the design phase, the safety case forces a view that is linked to accident scenarios, rather than a discipline-specific view of individual systems (process, mechanical, electrical, structural etc). With this in mind, information from field personnel about current work practices is a key safety case input. An understanding of the role that personnel in each part of the organisation play in preventing major disasters is a key output of the safety case process. Regulatory audits sometimes cover this aspect of accident prevention specifically to check that all personnel understand how their work impacts long-term facility safety.

(3) Risk acceptability (and so the need for further risk reduction) is based on the principle that risk must be reduced to ALARP.

What this means in the case of a pipeline is that additional controls must be put in place to mitigate every threat to pipeline integrity until it can be explicitly argued that the cost of further work is grossly disproportionate to the risk reduction that would be obtained. As described in Chapter 5, inspection (for example) cannot be constrained in the first instance by the available funds. To put it another way, to meet the requirement that risk is ALARP, companies cannot use capacity to pay as an argument not to take action that is justified on safety grounds, if the cost is reasonable when compared with the safety benefit. Rather, an argument that a proposed or an existing suite of risk controls is sufficient must be based on issues such as:

(a) the assessed level of risk in absolute terms (the higher the risk, the more additional controls are likely to be justified);

(b) the magnitude of the consequences if things do go wrong (while risk, ie frequency x consequence, is the primary determinant of the need for further action, it is common to give more weight to those risks that pose the worst consequences);

(c) whether the current/proposed risk control measures are consistent with industry best practice (if there are additional accepted measures such as those in industry standards that could be put in place, then there will need to be an argument as to why they are not also proposed in any particular case);

(d) the novelty of technology (more novel technology may have uncertainty associated with it and so a more conservative approach to risk control may be justified);

(e) the cost of additional risk controls, including initial and ongoing effort (cost can be taken into account but only as one factor among others);

(f) the degree to which the situation is inherently safe (preference should be given to controls that eliminate or mitigate threats, rather than those that attempt to contain impacts). This means, for new developments in particular, priority should be given to the lowest-risk design options; and

(g) for existing facilities, the demonstrated performance of existing controls (providing data on the effectiveness of existing controls can be part of a case that they are sufficient).

(4) The output of the process must be linked to the performance of actual risk controls in the field.

The final critical principle of the risk assessment component of a safety case is that the risk assessment is not the end in itself. The output of the process is an understanding of the most important risk controls that must be in place and the performance that is required of those controls. It is this last aspect that makes safety cases so powerful as a regulatory tool, since it provides a firm basis for enforcement activity.

The second component of a safety case is the safety management system. Such systems are based on quality management principles grounded in the well-known Deming cycle or feedback loop, consisting of four steps — Plan (establish goals and objectives), Do (implement processes), Check (measure output against goals), Act (act to improve performance) — which are seen as sequential, cyclic stages that operate at every level of the management system, from individual processes to the system as a whole.[11] Safety management system standards often advocate the same cyclic approach to performance improvement as the quality cycle described above, and no doubt the implementation of management system principles has helped many organisations to focus on and improve their overall safety performance.

Since this approach to ensuring worker (and public) safety has been so widely adopted, it might be expected that it has been shown to be effective in reducing injuries or fatalities. To date, it has been very difficult to make an objective determination regarding the effectiveness of safety case style regulation. If this approach is successful, then the ultimate benefit should be shown in improved safety performance but, since serious incidents are relatively rare, statistical conclusions are difficult to draw in any industry where other environmental factors are constantly changing. Several studies have attempted this exercise and all have

Chapter

9

tentatively reported positive results based primarily on qualitative, rather than quantitative, arguments.[12]

While objective evidence is somewhat ambiguous, there is no doubt that operating under a safety case regime has increased the attention paid to safety within industry. Hale et al[13] describe the benefit of 10 years of risk-based regulation for the petroleum industry in Holland as: "… companies have become more risk aware, safety cases and safety management systems are positive developments and there is more understanding of how and why risk control and management measures work." A major benefit of the safety case regime comes from the ongoing conversation about safety and engagement with safety-related issues within industry, especially relating to relatively rare events that would otherwise generate little discussion.

It is also important to remember that a risk-based safety regime does not eliminate the need for a competent and well-resourced regulatory agency, as we shall discuss further below. Before that, we compare the structure of the US pipeline regulations with the goal-setting approach described above.

US regulatory framework for pipeline safety

Having established what a goal-setting approach to pipeline safety regulation would look like in general terms, we now turn to the situation in the US. The technical integrity of the lines that failed was regulated by a US law known as Federal 49 CFR Part 192. These regulations fall within the jurisdiction of the US Department of Transportation, in particular, the Pipeline and Hazardous Materials Safety Administration (PHMSA). The PHMSA does not directly oversee PG&E's compliance with the regulations. Because this system is totally contained within the state of California, that role falls to the California Public Utilities Commission (CPUC). As will be described below, the problems related to the regulatory control of the integrity of line 132 are linked to both regulatory policy (primarily the responsibility of the PHMSA) and regulatory oversight (primarily the responsibility of the CPUC). Because Enbridge's pipelines cross several states, their US activities are overseen directly by the PHMSA.

In some ways, US law for the regulation of pipelines is superficially similar to a goal-setting regime in that it is a process-based regulation referring to a risk-based standard, but the US arrangement varies from the goal-setting model in several key aspects.

First of all, the overall intention of the regulatory regime for pipelines is quite different. In a goal-setting regime, the overall duty placed on operators is to reduce risk to ALARP. In contrast, Federal 49 CFR Part 192 is prescriptive and sets a minimum standard, as is made clear even in the title — Part 192 Transportation of

Natural and Other Gas by Pipeline: Minimum Federal Safety Standards. Section 192.1 describes the scope of Part 192 as "... prescribes minimum safety requirements for pipeline facilities and the transportation of gas ...". The overall duty of persons operating a pipeline is described in section 192.13 which states that "No person may operate a segment of pipeline ... unless ... the pipeline has been designed, installed, constructed, initially inspected, and initially tested in accordance with this part". So, rather than a legislative regime that aims to protect the public and requires the pipeline licensee to demonstrate that risk is ALARP, the US framework aims to set minimum standards and requires pipeline operators to meet those standards.*

Moving to integrity management planning in particular, section 192.907 requires that an operator:

> "... must develop and follow a written integrity management program that contains all the elements described in § 192.911 and that addresses the risks on each covered transmission pipeline segment. The initial integrity management program must consist, at a minimum, of a framework that describes the process for implementing each program element, how relevant decisions will be made and by whom, a time line for completing the work to implement the program element, and how information gained from experience will be continuously incorporated into the program. The framework will evolve into a more detailed and comprehensive program. An operator must make continual improvements to the program."

These requirements are similar to the Deming cycle described earlier. Further, the integrity management program must follow the requirements of a particular industry standard.[14] As explained in the introduction to the standard, it is based on the view that all operators are aiming for an ultimate goal of "incident-free operation", and the role of the standard is to assist "pipeline operators to move closer to that goal". The process described in the standard is risk-based: "The ultimate goal of assessing risks is to identify the most significant risks so that an operator can develop an effective and prioritized prevention/detection/mitigation plan to address the risks."[15]

It can be seen then that both the US regulations and the standard to which they refer assume a model of safety performance improvement based on quality management

---

* The discussion here is limited to the Federal safety regulations specifically. The CPUC is currently running a penalty consideration case against PG&E that links to a range of other legislation, including the California Public Utilities Code, section 451. This code requires all public utilities to provide and maintain "adequate, efficient, just, and reasonable" service and facilities as are necessary for the "safety, health, comfort, and convenience" of its customers and the public. PG&E is disputing its applicability and, for the purposes of this analysis, this separate legal action has been ignored as it clearly played no role in the oversight activities of the CPUC before the incident or in PG&E's understanding of its compliance obligations.

principles where overall objectives are set (in this case, to reduce incidents), work is done in accordance with documented processes, performance is assessed, and improvements made. This, again, is the well-known Plan-Do-Check-Act cycle and is very similar to the process described in any management system standard. This view that the function of risk assessment processes was to establish priorities for work, rather than to reach any conclusion about system adequacy in absolute terms, is demonstrated by the testimony of several PG&E staff at the NTSB hearing. As PG&E's Manager of Integrity Management said, "... when I say high risk, again these are terms of art in industry which do not mean that the high risk segments are going to fail. I know that that's tough to accept in the context of our conversation, but it means — you know, risk analysis is a way of focusing our attention on the pipelines that most need them. So it's a tool that we use on prioritization".[16] Her more senior colleague, the Director of Integrity Management, confirmed, "so when we calculate the risk it's for ... the establishment of the scheduling of the work".[17] When requirements for risk assessment are merged with management system concepts of continuous improvement, there is no requirement to demonstrate that the current level of risk is satisfactory or acceptable. The process establishes priorities, but not the urgency with which changes are required. Under this system, nothing is ever unacceptable!

More about management systems

As we have described, management systems are one of two primary components of a safety case. A management system approach is also a key aspect of US regulations and pipeline standards. Given this similarity, are these two ways of conceptualising safety really so different? The answer is a resounding "yes"! There are two important ways in which a management system approach differs from a safety case. The first is that a management system has no maximum acceptable level of risk, and second, it gives users no assistance in how to deal with conflicting goals, ie how to manage the balance between cost and safety.

To make this key point again, the problem lies in the overarching framework of the management system as continuous improvement. In a safety case regime, the first requirement is a risk assessment to demonstrate that risk is ALARP. Once the risk controls are in place, the safety management system kicks in to ensure that safety continues to improve. If this first step is missing, the process of continuing to improve is based on quicksand. Risk may be so high as to be completely unacceptable by any objective standard, and yet the proponents of the management system are able to say, "yes, but the risk is improving".

Some people argue that safety must always be the first priority and that cost should never be a consideration when it comes to safety. In this way of thinking, a safety management system can exist in isolation from the consideration of cost. The irony here is that, by failing to incorporate any formal consideration of cost, cost in fact prevails. It has been suggested that all that is needed to bring this approach into line with best practice is to impose a level of risk that is intolerable. This kind of scheme would involve continuous improvement, provided risk could be demonstrated as not beyond a defined tolerable level. Putting aside the problems with defining such a thing and then demonstrating that the actual risk is indeed below that level, this approach still treats safety in isolation and so is doomed to manipulation. It does not solve the fundamental problem that cost and safety are intimately intertwined and ultimately must be explicitly considered together. This is the major advantage of a regulatory regime based on demonstrating that risk is controlled as far as is reasonably practicable.

As highlighted earlier, the origin of this approach is quality management. These ideas have been responsible for major improvements in organisational production efficiencies — faster production of higher-quality products with less wastage — but the fact that this approach to safety performance gives no hints as to how to manage conflicting organisational goals is a serious gap. Prior to the loss of the *Columbia* space shuttle in February 2003, NASA management had adopted an organisational philosophy based on quality principles that it called "faster, better, cheaper". The concept of "better" as promoted within NASA did not include seeking improvements to safety. The goal of organisational safety was external to this management philosophy and was spoken of as "a constraint to be observed rather than a goal to be pursued".[18] This kind of thinking was a contributor to the circumstances that led to the loss of the space shuttle and it remains problematic.

The management system approach to pipeline safety in the US continues to be promoted. As part of the overall response to the Marshall accident, the NTSB asked the American Petroleum Institute (API) to facilitate the production of a safety management system standard for pipelines. The result is the recently released API *Recommended Practice 1173 Pipeline Safety Management System Requirements*. The process described in this document is again based on the Plan-Do-Check-Act cycle. Risk assessment is included as the way of identifying safety issues and setting priorities, and it includes some basic information about the importance of people, as well as technology, in excellent safety outcomes. There is no doubt that, had an effective system of this kind been in place, then both the PG&E and the Enbridge failures would have been less likely to occur. Our overarching issues with the process described are that, again, it is based on continuous improvement with no consideration of acceptable risk and it does not address how to manage the cost/safety trade-off.

These major flaws in adopting an approach to safety regulation grounded on a management system approach are also linked to the issue of "grandfathering", as discussed in Chapter 3 with regard to maximum allowable operating pressure determination and hydrotesting. Grandfathering is the process of providing a blanket exemption for old facilities from the requirements of updated standards. The reason that old facilities are exempted from meeting new requirements is the potential cost of compliance. As we have already stated, cost alone cannot be used as a reason for not making safety improvements under an ALARP-based duty of care regulatory regime. When the duty is founded on the ALARP principle, there is no blanket answer to the issue of new standards and old equipment. This question must be answered on a case-by-case basis. There is no blanket requirement to upgrade, but neither is there a blanket exemption. Costs and risks must be balanced, and changes made to improve equipment if the cost is reasonable compared to the benefit gained — taking into account the newest knowledge about the risks involved.

Auditing and effective enforcement

Any regulatory regime requires effective enforcement. Even in the best regulatory agencies, resources are limited and a clearly articulated enforcement strategy is needed to ensure that effort is expended consistently and effectively. This is partly a question of the tools provided in legislation. A useful way to think about how best to influence companies to comply with regulation is to see enforcement tools as a set of graduated steps with increasing severity if compliance is not achieved by actions lower on the scale.[19] At the bottom lie education, awareness-raising and safety promotion activities on the part of the regulator. In the middle are audits and inspections, with formal notices issued for significant issues found. If companies still persist in non-compliance despite formal notices, an effective regulatory regime will have tools available at the top of the scale that have further financial and reputational penalties, such as fines, prosecution and/or withdrawal of permission to operate facilities. These would only be used rarely in cases where other measures have failed, but it is important for all stakeholders to know that such penalties can and will be used if necessary. It should be noted that these enforcement actions are primarily about gaining compliance, not punishing companies post-accident.

In a goal-setting regulatory regime, companies are audited by regulators against requirements that they themselves have set. The regulator will also tap into the company auditing process and outcomes as part of this program — the company should be auditing itself far more regularly than the regulator can physically achieve. This requires regulators with a high degree of technical knowledge and experience. In the case of PG&E, it was the responsibility of the CPUC to monitor compliance and the main tool in use was auditing. PG&E's integrity management program was audited in the fourth quarter of 2005 and again in May 2010. The first issue of note is the five-year gap between audits on this critical system.[20]

Looking first at the 2005 audit report, the focus was on whether PG&E's systems and procedures complied with the requirements of the regulations and the relevant standard (ASME B31.8S[14]). There appears to be little, if any, direct assessment of whether the inspection activity is effective at managing system integrity. The 138-page report includes an assessment of compliance with dozens of specific requirements, with each one rated "no issues", "potential issues identified", or "not applicable". The results show that, in over 50 cases, the auditors found that the PG&E system was potentially not in compliance. The report includes no assessment of the potential consequences of these breaches. PG&E claims never to have received any consolidated feedback on this audit and yet some of the "potential issues identified" listed in the report appear to be quite serious, reflecting, for example, some of the flaws in the overall integrity management system listed in Chapter 5. PG&E's Director of Integrity Management called the four-page summary received in the exit interview at the end of the audit as "a smorgasbord of comments", suggesting that PG&E was unsure which ones required action, if any.[21]

Given that the next audit of PG&E's integrity management system was conducted five years later, it seems reasonable to assume that the regulator was of the view that these 2005 breaches were not particularly serious. Otherwise, it might be expected that resources would be allocated for follow-up and for further enforcement if PG&E had taken no action. The results of the next audit in May 2010 were not formally issued to PG&E until 21 October 2010, ie more than four months after the audit and six weeks after the San Bruno pipeline rupture. The audit again identified many shortcomings which are summarised in the cover letter: "PG&E is diluting the requirements of its IMP [integrity management plan] through its exception process and appears to be allocating insufficient resources to carry out and complete assignments in a timely manner."[22] Of course, this was written with knowledge of the incident which had recently occurred, but simply flags that the regulator knew of significant problems at PG&E before the accident, but took no effective action.

So, in summary, the CPUC auditing regime did not include sufficient field audits. It also did not prioritise the identified non-conformances and did not follow up non-conformances to ensure that they were acted on. In this way, no escalation of enforcement action was triggered by the audit findings or response.

Returning again to the style of safety regulation that the CPUC was trying to enforce, the requirements regarding integrity management in ASME B31.8S[14] are again based on the Plan-Do-Check-Act management system cycle. The outputs of such a standard may very well be a better fit for purpose for each pipeline system, but they are harder to audit than a set of standard prescriptive requirements that apply universally. As the NTSB reported, the regulator found this task difficult:[23]

"The PHMSA deputy associate administrator for policy and programs testified at the NTSB investigative hearing that performance-based regulations such as the integrity management rules are very difficult for operators to implement and for regulators to oversee because there is no 'one-size-fits-all answer to integrity issues'. She stated that, 'every operator is expected to thoroughly understand their system' and 'assess for the threats to that pipe … then you must address them'. She noted that overseeing operator compliance with the integrity management rules is very different from overseeing compliance with more clear-cut prescriptive regulations because 'now they are required to think in a totally different manner. They have to evaluate the adequacy of an operator's technical justification. It is difficult. It's a difficult way of evaluating a program, but it's effective'."

The other key factor that makes it difficult to prioritise non-compliances in such a system is the fact that, as we have already described above, it is based on the concept of continuous improvement. Using this argument in reverse simply means that, if something that should be in place is missing, then performance is less than it could be, but it is never judged to be unacceptable or too dangerous. We believe that this is also a significant factor in the regulators' difficulties when dealing with a host of non-compliances identified at PG&E in 2005.

Regulation is a profession in itself. Competent and effective regulators operate in accordance with a clear regulatory philosophy to protect workers and the public. If this valuable work is not seen in these terms, it is almost bound to be ineffective.

Conclusion

Ultimately, without standards and regulations that allow regulators to say *before an accident occurs* that a facility or an activity is unsafe, there can be no effective regulatory regime. This requires a regime that is based on a general duty to reduce risk to ALARP, not simply a requirement for continuous improvement. Continuous improvement is admirable, but only if risk is at an acceptable level to start with. For this reason, regulations that require risk-based management systems alone are not sufficient.

Much has been written about the need for well-resourced, competent regulators in duty of care regulatory regimes and the separation of safety regulation from industry promotion functions.[24] Without this, any regulatory agency runs the risk of "regulatory capture"; in other words, no longer holding industry to account on behalf of the public and workers, but rather taking on a viewpoint that is overly sympathetic to industry needs. In this case, the US regulatory arrangement appears to have been lacking in both policy and implementation, with a regime that effectively led to PG&E operating in an unregulated manner for years prior to the rupture. As this book goes to press, further allegations of a close and inappropriate relationship between the CPUC and PG&E have surfaced.[25] This only goes to emphasise the need for widespread regulatory reform in the US — both at a policy level and at the level of implementation and enforcement.

We have included some additional comments regarding US regulatory approaches in Chapter 10 in the context of a discussion about the merits of compliance as a safety strategy.

Endnotes

1   Haukelid, K, "Theories of (safety) culture revisited — an anthropological approach", *Safety Science* 2008, 46: 413–426.

2   Cullen, WD, *The public inquiry into the Piper Alpha disaster*, HMSO, London, 1990.

3   Paterson, J, *Behind the mask: regulating health and safety in Britain's offshore oil and gas industry*, Ashgate, Aldershot, 2000.

4   Hale, A, Goossens, L and Van de Poel, I, "Oil and gas industry regulation: from detailed technical inspection to assessment of safety management", in Kirwan, B, Hale, A and Hopkins, A (eds), *Changing regulation: controlling risks in society*, Pergamon, Oxford, 2002.

5   Kirwan, B, Hale, A and Hopkins, A, "Insights into safety regulation", in Kirwan, B, Hale, A and Hopkins, A (eds), *Changing regulation: controlling risks in society*, Pergamon, Oxford, 2002.

6   Maurino, D, Reason, J, Johnston, N and Lee, R, *Beyond aviation human factors*, Ashgate, Aldershot, 1995.

     McIntyre, GR, *Patterns in safety thinking: a literature guide to air transportation safety*, Ashgate, Aldershot, 2000.

7   Schobel, M, "Compliance with safety rules: the role of environmental structures", in Itoigawa, N, Wilpert, B and Fahlbruch, B (eds), *Emerging demands for the safety of nuclear power operations*, CRC Press, Boca Raton, 2005.

     Williams, J, "New frontiers for regulatory interaction within the UK nuclear industry", in Kirwan, B, Hale, A and Hopkins, A (eds) *Changing regulation: controlling risks in society*, Pergamon, Oxford, 2002.

8   Hopkins, A, "Two models of major hazard regulation: recent Australian experience", in Kirwan, B, Hale, A and Hopkins, A (eds), *Changing regulation: controlling risks in society*, Pergamon, Oxford, 2002.

     Oh, JIH, "The EU Seveso II Directive: an example of a regulation that could act as an initiator to raise the major hazard safety awareness within society", in Kirwan, B, Hale, A and Hopkins, A (eds), *Changing regulation: controlling risks in society*, Pergamon, Oxford, 2002.

9   Hale, AR, Heijer, T and Koornneef, F, "Management of safety rules: the case of the railways", *Safety Science Monitor* 2003, 7(1): 1–11.

10   Quoted in Bluff, L and Johnstone, R, *The relationship between "reasonably practicable" and risk management regulation*, working paper 27, National Research Centre for OHS Regulation, Canberra, 2004. Available at http://regnet.anu.edu.au/publications/wp-27-relationship-between-reasonably-practicable-and-risk-management-regulation.

11   Deming, WE, *Out of the crisis*, MIT Press, Cambridge, 2000.

12　HSE, *An interim evaluation of the Offshore Installation (Safety Case) Regulations 1992*, HSE, Norwich, 1995.

　　HSE, *Literature review on the perceived benefits and disadvantages of UK safety case regimes*, HSE, Norwich, 2003.

　　Rose, D and Crescent, J, *Evaluation of the offshore safety legislative regime in the UK*, Society of Petroleum Engineers International Conference on Health, Safety, and the Environment in Oil and Gas Exploration and Production, Stavanger, Norway, 26 to 28 June 2000.

　　VECTRA, *Literature review of the perceived benefits and disadvantages of the UK safety case regimes*, HSE, London, 2003.

　　Vinnem, JE, "Analysis of root causes of major hazard precursors in the Norwegian offshore petroleum industry", *Reliability Engineering and System Safety*, 2010 (accepted manuscript).

　　Hopkins, A, *The cost benefit hurdle for safety case regulation*, working paper 88, National Research Centre for OHS Regulation, Canberra, 2014. Available at http://regnet.anu.edu.au/publications/wp-88-cost-benefit-hurdle-safety-case-regulation.

13　Hale, A, Goossens, L and Van de Poel, I, "Oil and gas industry regulation: from detailed technical inspection to assessment of safety management", in Kirwan, B, Hale, A and Hopkins, A (eds), *Changing regulation: controlling risks in society*, Pergamon, Oxford, 2002.

14　American Society of Mechanical Engineers, *B31.8S Managing system integrity of gas pipelines*, 2012.

15　American Society of Mechanical Engineers, p 2.

16　NTSB Accident Docket DCA10MP008, Document 218, *Public Hearing Transcript - March 1, 2011 (Day One)*, p 86. Available at http://dms.ntsb.gov/pubdms/search/document.cfm?docID=344892&docketID=49896&mkey=77250.

17　NTSB, ibid, p 152.

18　Ocasio, W, "The opacity of risk: language and the culture of safety in NASA's space shuttle program", in Starbuck, WH and Farjoun, M (eds), *Organization at the limit: lessons from the Columbia disaster*, Blackwell, Malden, Massachusetts, 2005, p 108.

19　Ayres, I and Braithwaite, J, *Responsive regulation: transcending the deregulation debate*, Oxford University Press, New York, 1992.

20　We are not aware of any consolidated published data on regulatory audit or inspection frequency, but our work with several regulatory agencies suggests that this is a much longer interval than would be expected from a well-resourced and competent regulatory agency.

21　*Pipeline safety since San Bruno and other incidents*, hearing before the Subcommittee on Surface Transportation and Merchant Marine Infrastructure, Safety, and Security of the Committee on Commerce, Science and Transportation, United States Senate, Washington DC, 18 October 2011, p 22, line 7.

22　CPUC, letter to PG&E (regarding May 2010 integrity management program audit), 21 October 2010, p 1. Available at www.cpuc.ca.gov/NR/rdonlyres/18FD46B2-298E-46AF-99E9-BD75A419BB10/0/2010AuditofPGEIMP.pdf.

23　NTSB, *Pacific Gas and Electric Company natural gas transmission pipeline rupture and fire, San Bruno, CA, September 9, 2010,* pipeline accident report, Washington DC, 2011, p 70.

24　Hale, A, Borys, D and Adams, M, "Safety regulation: the lessons of workplace safety rule management for managing the regulatory burden", *Safety Science*, DOI: 10.1016/j.ssci.2013.11.012 (in press).

Hayes, J, "A new direction in offshore safety regulation", in Baram, M, Lindoe, P and Renn, O (eds), *Governing risk in offshore oil and gas operations*, Cambridge University Press, Cambridge, 2013.

Hopkins, A, "Beyond compliance monitoring: new strategies for safety regulators", *Law and Policy* 2007, 29(2): 210–225.

Hopkins, A, *Explaining safety case*, working paper 87, National Research Centre for OHS Regulation, Canberra, 2013. Available at http://regnet.anu.edu.au/publications/wp-87-explaining-%E2%80%9Csafety-case%E2%80%9D.

Kirwan, B, Hale, A and Hopkins, A, "Insights into safety regulation", in Kirwan, B, Hale, A and Hopkins, A (eds), *Changing regulation: controlling risks in society*, Pergamon, Oxford, 2002.

Paterson, J, *Behind the mask: regulating health and safety in Britain's offshore oil and gas industry*, Ashgate, Aldershot, 2000.

25   Knickmeyer, E and Blood, M, "PG&E emails may have violated rules, judge says", *The Washington Times*, 18 September 2014.

Roberts, K and Schulman, P, "PUC, PG&E should be allies, not adversaries, on safety", *San Francisco Chronicle*, 19 August 2014.

Chapter

9

CHAPTER 10

THE COMPLIANCE PARADOX

This book embodies a paradox. One of the causes of the Marshall accident was the failure of operators to comply with rules. On the other hand, one of the causes of the San Bruno accident, and of the Marshall accident, was the focus on compliance with prescriptive regulatory rules, *at the expense of safety*. Such a focus is sometimes described as a "compliance mentality". This description heightens the sense of paradox: in the Marshall case, operator compliance would have been a good thing, while in both cases, a "compliance mentality" in relation to regulation was part of the problem. Chapter 10 explores this paradox and, we hope, resolves it. In the process, we necessarily revisit some of the matters discussed in Chapter 9. But in so doing, we generalise that discussion. For a start, Chapter 10 is not just concerned with externally imposed rules, but also with rules and procedures that companies make for themselves. The chapter is also concerned with major hazard regulation in the United States generally, not just in the pipeline industry. In the process, it seeks to contribute further to the current debate in the US about the need for performance-based, as opposed to prescriptive, regulation.

Prescriptive rules

Prescriptive rules have much to recommend them. They may be based on past experience — what went wrong — and embody ways of ensuring that this does not happen again. Such a rule is a manifestation of organisational or system learning. For example, various companies have analysed previous fatalities and formulated rules which, if observed, would have prevented the fatalities, such as rules about driving, working at heights, and working in confined spaces. These are variously known as life-saving rules, golden rules, cardinal rules, and so on, and they are often vigorously enforced.

Or again, take the issue of safe operating limits. It may require complex calculations to determine what these are, but the end point of this process is a rule which plant operators must follow, blindly, since they may have little understanding about the way in which the operating rules were determined. This situation illustrates nicely the interdependence of prescriptive rules and risk management. The operator is faced with a prescriptive rule to comply with, but that rule may have been developed on the basis of a complex risk assessment process.[1]

Prescriptive rules do however have their drawbacks. If they turn out to be impractical, people will be tempted to ignore them, or devise their own work-arounds. Some authors applaud such an outcome. According to Klein, "skilled performers need latitude to depart from procedures".[2] However, as described in Chapter 4, departures from procedure may be an indication of the inadequacy of the procedure. Moreover, departures from the procedure may increase the risk in ways that operators do not understand. A great many disasters have been triggered by skilled operators deviating from procedures, and doing so routinely, because of the perceived inadequacy of the procedure.[3] Where skilled operators identify aspects of procedures that in their minds require them to depart from strict compliance, this needs to be highlighted so that the procedures can be reconsidered and theory and practice more closely aligned.

This last point is vital: prescriptive rule regimes must be actively managed by those who formulate the rules. Two aspects of management are particularly important: monitoring and response to non-compliance.[4] Rule formulators must monitor behaviour to ensure that people are complying with the rules. Where non-compliance is detected, there must be a response. If the non-compliance is a result of the inappropriateness or inapplicability of the rule, the rule must be changed. This means that there must be a rule modification procedure that incorporates both the experience of those to whom the rule applies, as well as the intentions of the rule-makers. On the other hand, if the non-compliance stems from ignorance or simply a lack of commitment, then education or disciplinary consequences may be appropriate.

Another often-mentioned problem with prescriptive rules is that they do not take account of changing circumstances and changing technologies. Regulations governing coal mines in Australia contained provisions on the stabling of horses underground, many decades after the use of horses had been discontinued! Here, again, the solution is an active rule management system.

A third problem is that the activity that the rules are designed to cover may require such a high degree of professional judgment that it is inappropriate to try to control it using detailed prescriptive rules. It may nevertheless be useful to develop guidelines to assist professionals who are new to this particular activity and, indeed, to serve as a prompt to old hands. Such guidelines are then better seen as a statement of the practice of professionals with long experience, rather than rules that must be followed. This distinction between guidelines and rules became critical in a commission of inquiry into the way engineers operated flood control gates on the Wivenhoe Dam during a flood disaster in Queensland.[5] The Commission acknowledged that the engineers achieved a near-perfect outcome in the circumstances, yet criticised them severely for not following the flood mitigation manual to the letter. The response of the engineers was that the manual is "simply a description of what people had always done in making operational decisions", not a document that they followed slavishly. Unfortunately, the manual, while originally prepared as guidance, was subsequently approved by government and so took on a different status. The requirement, at least in the Commission's view, for black letter compliance led to a great deal of confusion and unwarranted criticism.

It might be thought that the activity of some professionals, such as surgeons, is so complex that it cannot be proceduralised at all. In some respects, this is true. Nevertheless, experience has shown that highly prescriptive procedural rules can be of great value, even in this context. Where surgeons are required to follow procedural checklists designed to reduce medical errors and iatrogenic infections, patient survival rates are much improved.[6] These outcomes demonstrate that procedural rules can be workable and very valuable, even where the principal activity cannot be reduced to prescriptive action rules.

A digression on expertise

The preceding discussion begs the question, what is an expert? It is worth saying a few words on this subject so as to bring out aspects of the relationship between rules and expertise. Some expertise is built up by years of on-the-job experience. It can be described as tacit knowledge,[7] difficult to specify and difficult to communicate to others but vital for safe and effective operation. Almost by definition, such tacit knowledge is difficult, if not impossible, to reduce to rules. Much has been written, for instance, about coal miners and their ability to interpret the noises made by the roof and the timbers that support it, and to know when the roof may be about to fall. Operators of process equipment such as pipelines develop this kind of expertise over time. Klein describes decision-making based on this kind of expertise as "recognition-primed decision-making".[8] It involves comparing the situation that confronts them with others they have experienced and drawing conclusions on this basis.

But there is a crucial limitation to such expertise. Since is it based on experience, it is of no value when dealing with catastrophic events that may be so rare that they are beyond the experience of seasoned personnel. A classic illustration occurred on the *Deepwater Horizon* drilling rig prior to the blowout in the Gulf of Mexico in 2010. The drillers were experienced men, highly skilled at what they did. However, when certain test results revealed that the well was at risk of blowing out, they failed to recognise the significance of the results and fatally misinterpreted them. Where experts, whose knowledge is based on on-the-job experience, are dealing with matters *beyond* their experience, it is desirable that their decision-making be determined by rules devised by others to take account of exceptional circumstances.

There is second kind of expertise, based on abstract knowledge rather than direct experience. The expertise of the dam engineers and the surgeons discussed above is of this second type. A distinctive feature of such expertise is that, when confronted with unprecedented situations, such experts may be able reason their way to an appropriate course of action, based on theoretical understanding and/or knowledge derived from the experience of others. Of course, there may also be elements of the first type of expertise — tacit, experience-based knowledge — involved in the performance of such experts.

Coincidentally, the Gulf of Mexico disaster provides an example of this second kind of expertise. Once the blowout occurred, it had to be stemmed and stopped. But a high-pressure blowout 1.5 km below sea level was an unprecedented problem. BP assembled its best engineers, and the US Government its best scientists, and together they worked through one option after another, until finally they arrived at an innovative strategy to control the flow and eventually plug the hole. This was a situation in which there were no rules to be followed; the decision-making process was necessarily governed by argument and evidence. It was by one account a formidable display of scientific and engineering expertise, and one of the few aspects of the accident in which humans performed at their best.[9] Klein has said that "in complex and ambiguous situations, there is no substitute for experience".[10] However, where the situation is unprecedented, there may be no substitute for deep thinking and abstract knowledge.

Parenthetically, we note that Reason talks about a similar kind of expertise in his discussion of "inspired innovation". His main examples are airline pilots who, when confronted with unprecedented failures, were able draw on deep theoretical knowledge to improvise life-saving solutions.[11]

The Enbridge operators

Let us now focus this discussion on the Marshall accident. The Enbridge operators frequently failed to comply with rules. The outstanding example was the 10-minute rule. This required operators to stop pumping if alarms could be not be resolved within 10 minutes. Had the operators complied with this rule, the scale of the release would have been much less. It turns out that operators were accustomed to exceeding the 10-minute restriction, indicating that the non-compliance on this occasion was the norm, not the exception. For this reason, among others, the official accident report spoke of a "culture of deviance", a "culture that accepted not adhering to the procedures". This culture came about for two reasons. The first is that the rules themselves were sometimes inappropriate and/or ambiguous, which encouraged operators to develop their own working rules. The second reason is that Enbridge had no process for monitoring compliance. It formulated the rules and then left compliance up to the operators, in effect, making compliance optional. Had there been a system of monitoring compliance, the culture of deviance would have come to light long before the accident. As it was, operators used their own expertise to guide their decisions. Given that their expertise was limited, their decisions were correspondingly flawed. So it was that failure to comply with procedures was a major contributing factor to the scale of the Marshall release.

A compliance mentality

The issue we now need to confront is how a focus on rule compliance can sometimes amount to something undesirable — a compliance mentality. The problem is that, while prescriptive safety rules are designed to promote safety, they are likely to be defective in some respects and, in any case, can never cover every contingency. Safety therefore depends not just on compliance with rules, but also on maintaining a level of risk awareness that goes beyond mere compliance. This is readily illustrated with road safety. Even though you comply with all road safety rules, you may still suffer an accident as a result of your own failure to anticipate changed road conditions or as a result of someone else's driving. A higher-level of safety can be achieved by defensive driving, in which you seek to anticipate and allow for the unexpected. Defensive driving involves being continuously aware of risk and engaging in various risk management strategies, such as watching the brake lights of the car two ahead of you in a stream of traffic so as to reduce the risk of being involved in a pile up. To believe that compliance with road safety rules is sufficient to guarantee one's safety is clearly misguided; it amounts to a compliance mentality that has lost sight of the primary goal — road safety. Similarly, compliance with prescriptive industrial safety rules is not enough to guarantee industrial safety, and a narrow focus on compliance with prescriptive rules may produce a compliance mentality on the part of individuals and organisations that loses sight of safety. Indeed, compliance may become a ritual where compliance with the letter of the rule, rather than its spirit, becomes all that matters.

Our earlier discussion of the San Bruno accident provided a clear example of the problem. The pipeline had been exempted from the legal requirement that it be hydrotested because it would have needed to be taken out of service for such a test. Instead, it was allowed to operate up to the maximum pressure at which it had operated in the previous five years. PG&E exploited this situation by periodically increasing the pressure in the line up to this limit, so that it could legally continue operating up to that pressure. This amounted to the worst kind of ritualistic compliance. We say this because the procedure actually increased the risk of failure over time, and arguably contributed to the San Bruno failure. Another remarkable example, discussed in Chapter 6, was Enbridge's cathodic protection system for corrosion control. The system was maintained, even on sections of pipeline where it was known to be ineffective, simply to comply with regulatory requirements.

Various examples of this compliance mentality came to light in the Gulf of Mexico disaster. To mention just one, the last line of defence to the blowout was the blowout preventer — a large piece of machinery sitting on the sea floor. This was supposed to be able to shear through the drill pipe in an emergency and close off the well. When called on to perform this function to prevent the Gulf of Mexico blowout, it failed. In the circumstances, this failure was not at all surprising, as we show in what follows.

Consider the way that blowout preventers (BOPs) were tested.[12] There are many types of test that can be done on a complex piece of equipment like this. The ultimate test is to ask it to perform its emergency function in circumstances that are as close as possible to those that will prevail in the emergency. This is time-consuming and expensive. A study done for the regulator in 2002 found that, of six BOPs that were tested in this way, only three succeeded in shearing the drill pipe. This is a failure rate of 50%.[13] It is also possible to test individual components of a BOP without calling on it to cut through pipe in the conditions that exist on the sea floor. An example would be testing whether electrical circuits are functioning as intended. The regulator required a large number of such tests and they were almost always successful — there were only 62 failures out of nearly 90,000 tests conducted over several years.[14] In short, while realistic testing of the ability of BOPs to function in an emergency yielded an alarming failure rate of 50%, the more limited forms of testing prescribed by the regulator suggested that BOPs functioned in a very reliable way. This discrepancy seemed not to matter, however, because what was uppermost in everyone's mind was regulatory compliance, not safety. The testing regime had lost sight of safety. One is reminded again of the drunk searching for his keys under a street light. We have already used this metaphor in Chapter 5 for a convenient method of integrity testing that has major limitations in that it only reveals problems with external corrosion and fails to address other potential integrity threats. In the same way, BOP tests were prescribed because they were relatively easy to do, not because they could provide the ultimate demonstration that a BOP would function as intended in an emergency.

Finally, we note that it is common for uninformed operators to defer to regulations and adopt a compliance mentality because they assume that, if they were required to do more, then it would be within the regulations. Prescriptive regulations promote this mentality.

In principle, a compliance mentality is less likely to be found where rules are part of an active and flexible rule management program. Such a program will encourage people to be alert to situations where the rules are not achieving the best and safest outcomes and to notify rule-makers of the discrepancy.[15] Interestingly, an active rule management program both relies on and encourages risk awareness that goes beyond mere compliance. Companies may devise such rule management regimes for themselves, but governments and regulators have much greater difficulty. Complex and cumbersome rule change procedures may delay necessary government rule changes for decades. An excellent example of this is the way that the offshore petroleum safety regulator in the US was thwarted for decades in its attempts to introduce a requirement for safety and environmental management systems in US waters.[16]

The absence of goal-oriented rules in the US

There is a particular feature of many regulatory regimes in the US that encourages companies to adopt a compliance mentality. Although there are often voluminous sets of prescriptive rules that regulators have formulated in an effort to maximise safety, there is no specific requirement that companies themselves seek to maximise safety. Where there is no regulatory requirement to maximise safety or minimise risk, companies almost inevitably will tend to focus their efforts on compliance rather than safety. This was demonstrated in some detail in Chapter 9 for pipeline regulation in the US.

There are some specialised goal-setting regimes in the US. For example, the National Aeronautics and Space Administration has the goal of implementing a safety system that is "as safe as reasonably practicable", while the Nuclear Regulatory Commission that overseas commercial nuclear power plants requires licensees to reduce risk to "as low as reasonably achievable".[17]

But the Occupational Safety and Health Act that covers much of US industry contains no such requirement.* Even the Occupational Safety and Health Administration (OSHA) process safety management (PSM) standard, which deals with many major hazard facilities, prescribes a process for managing safety rather than specifying safety as a goal. Let us develop this point briefly. The heart of the PSM standard is the following requirement:[18]

> "The employer shall perform an initial process hazard analysis (hazard evaluation) on processes covered by this standard. The process hazard

---

* Interestingly, there *is* a general duty under the US Occupational Safety and Health Act. Section 5(a)(1) of the Act specifies that employers must provide a workplace that is "free from recognized hazards that are causing or are likely to cause death or serious physical harm". This is radically different from the general duty to ensure safety so far as reasonably practicable. For a more detailed discussion, see Hopkins, A, *Explaining safety case*, working paper 87, National Research Centre for OHS Regulation, Canberra, 2013, pp 6–8. Available at http://regnet.anu.edu.au/publications/wp-87-explaining-%E2%80%9Csafety-case%E2%80%9D.

analysis shall be appropriate to the complexity of the process and shall identify, evaluate, and control the hazards involved in the process."

Further clauses provide considerable detail on just how this is to be carried out. But nowhere does the standard specify an outcome; nowhere does it say that risk must be as low as reasonably practicable, or words to that effect. Without such a requirement, and without a requirement that the operator demonstrate to the regulator that the risks are as low as reasonably practicable, there is no way to ensure that the response to the PSM standard is more than ritual compliance with the specified procedures.

This problem in US legislation is now in the spotlight. The Presidential Commission on the Gulf of Mexico accident recommended that offshore oil and gas production be regulated with a safety case regime that imposes an obligation on operators to reduce risk to as low as reasonably practicable. The report of the US Chemical Safety Board (CSB) on that same accident also recommended a safety case regime for the offshore industry. Moreover, following a major refinery fire in California, the CSB recommended to the state of California that it introduce safety case regulation for its onshore petroleum industry.[19] As we go to press, California has just proposed a novel standard for oil refineries that will require them to eliminate risk "to the greatest extent feasible".[20] Feasible is defined as "capable of being achieved". At first sight, this would appear to be a more stringent requirement than "as low as reasonably practicable". It will be interesting to see whether this proposed rule is promulgated and, if so, how it is interpreted. It is clear, however, that the winds of change are blowing in the US.

One of the benefits of a safety case regime that has not so far been mentioned is that it has the potential to reduce some of the antagonism that pervades the US system about whether particular rules apply or not. For example, some companies have resisted attempts by OSHA to get them to comply with the standards of the American Petroleum Institute, on the grounds that these are merely *recommended practices*.[21] Under a safety case regime, the issue is not whether certain standards are mandatory, but whether the risk is as low as reasonably practicable. It would be difficult for a company to claim that it did not intend to comply with a standard because it was merely a recommendation, and yet claim that it had reduced risks as far as reasonably practicable.

It is worth observing, finally, that not only does a compliance mentality fail to ensure safety, it also fails to provide immunity from legal liability when things go wrong. An organisation may be in compliance with all relevant regulations and still be found negligent if it failed to take additional steps that it might reasonably have been expected to take.[22] On the other hand, if it has reduced risk to as low as reasonably practicable, that is, it has taken all reasonable steps to minimise the risk, it is, ipso facto, not negligent.

Resolving the paradox

Let us return to the paradox which, like all paradoxes, is not really a paradox when properly understood. The notion of a "compliance mentality" suggests that compliance is a problem, in and of itself. That is not the case. The problem is that compliance may not be enough. The real culprit, then, is the "compliance is enough" mentality. This is known disparagingly in some circles as AHARA — as high as regulations allow. Where there are additional steps available to evaluate and control risk, the failure to take these additional steps amounts to dangerous risk blindness. It is a tragedy that US regulatory regimes have tended to encourage this kind of risk blindness.

Endnotes

1   Hopkins, A, "Risk-management and rule-compliance: decision-making in hazardous industries", *Safety Science* 2011, 49: 110–120.

2   Klein, GA, *Streetlights and shadows: searching for the keys to adaptive decision making*, MIT Press, Cambridge, Massachusetts, 2009, p 24.

3   Hopkins, A, *Failure to learn: the BP Texas City Refinery disaster*, CCH Australia Limited, Sydney, 2008, ch 2.

4   Hale, A and Borys, D, "Working to rule, or working safely? Part 1: a state of the art review", *Safety Science* 2013, 55: 207–221.

    Hale, A and Borys, D, "Working to rule, or working safely? Part 2: the management of safety rules and procedures", *Safety Science* 2013, 55: 222–231.

5   Maslen, S and Hayes, J, "Experts under the microscope: the Wivenhoe Dam case", *Environment Systems and Decisions* 2014, 34(2): 183–193.

6   Pronovost, P, *Safe patients, smart hospitals: how one doctor's checklist can help us change health care from the inside out*, Hudson, New York, 2010.

    Gawande, A, *The checklist manifesto*, Macmillan, 2010.

7   Polanyi, M, *The tacit dimension*, Doubleday, New York, 1967.

8   Klein, GA, *Streetlights and shadows: searching for the keys to adaptive decision making*, MIT Press, Cambridge, Massachusetts, 2009, pp 90–93.

9   Achenbach, J, *A hole at the bottom of the sea: the race to kill the BP Oil gusher*, Simon and Schuster, New York, 2011, especially ch 6.

10 Klein, GA, *Streetlights and shadows: searching for the keys to adaptive decision making*, MIT Press, Cambridge, Massachusetts, 2009, p 12.

11 Reason, J, *The human contribution: unsafe acts, accidents and heroic recoveries*, Ashgate, Farnham, 2008, pp 213ff and 225.

12 Hopkins, A, *Disastrous decisions: the human and organisational causes of the Gulf of Mexico blowout*, CCH Australia Limited, Sydney, 2012, p 142.

Chapter

10

13   West Engineering Services, *Mini shear study for US Minerals Management Service*, December 2002. See *New York Times*, oil spill documents.

14   West Engineering Services, *Blowout prevention equipment reliability joint industry project*. See *New York Times*, oil spill documents.

15   Bourrier, M, "Elements for designing a self-correcting organization: examples from nuclear power plants", in Hale, AR and Baram, M (eds), *Safety management: the challenge of change*, Pergamon, Oxford, 1998.

16   National Commission on the BP Deepwater Horizon Oil Spill and Offshore Drilling, *Deepwater: the Gulf oil disaster and the future of offshore drilling, report to the President*, 2011.

17   US Chemical Safety and Hazard Investigation Board, *Regulatory report: Chevron Richmond Refinery pipe rupture and fire*, report no. 2012-03-I-CA, May 2014, pp 35–36.

18   OSHA, *1910.119 Process safety management of highly hazardous chemicals*. See subsection (e)(1).

19   US Chemical Safety and Hazard Investigation Board, *Regulatory report: Chevron Richmond Refinery pipe rupture and fire*, report no. 2012-03-I-CA, May 2014.

20   Farley, M, "California proposes major changes to refinery process safety management (PSM) standard", *The National Law Review*, 19 September 2014. Available at www.natlawreview.com/article/california-proposes-major-changes-to-refinery-process-safety-management-psm-standard.

21   Hopkins, A, "Risk-management and rule-compliance: decision-making in hazardous industries", *Safety Science* 2011, 49: 110–120 at 116.

22   Weaver, J, "Offshore safety in the wake of the Macondo disaster: business as usual or a sea change?", *Houston Journal of International Law* Winter 2014: 147–216 at 166.

CHAPTER 11

CONCLUDING REMARKS

We have chosen to subtitle this book "fantasy planning, black swans and integrity management" because these are three key areas that we would like readers to think about in relation to their own organisations.

The circumstances that led to the San Bruno and Enbridge disasters had existed for many years and yet no one had acted to change them. Without dramatic evidence of a problem, it is easy for organisations to fall into the trap of fantasy planning — thinking that graphs, algorithms and models are not simply an attempt to approximate reality but that they *are* reality. Challenging organisational complacency and disrupting the organisational certainty that comes from long-held views that the system is safe is difficult but necessary if further catastrophes are to be avoided. We hope this book contributes to the diversity of views that is required to ensure that organisations are not carried away in their optimism.

Just as problematic is the "stuff happens" view of risk and disaster. Preventing black swans is difficult, but by looking in depth at how some organisations have got this wrong, we can see ways for all organisations to maintain a focus on disaster prevention. There is no excuse for a fatalistic view that in the end sees accidents as random events over which companies have little control.

Integrity management is an especially thankless task. When it is most effective, there is apparently little to see — pipelines that do not leak. It is hardly surprising that senior managers driven by profit are tempted to trim or even slash budgets. But, as we have seen in two companies, getting integrity management decisions wrong can be catastrophic. The saving grace for companies wishing to avoid the same fate is that there will be evidence of problems if only the organisation has the systems in place to find it and to ensure that decision-makers act accordingly.

Causes of the San Bruno pipeline rupture and fire

Eight people died when PG&E's line 132 failed and the suburb of San Bruno was effectively razed to the ground. In summary, we see the immediate causes of this event to be fourfold.

First, the accident would not have happened but for the faulty weld from 1956. While this was a significant fault, any background as to why it occurred or how the line came to be put in service incorporating such a flaw has been lost. The broader question is why this problem was not detected over the more than 50 years that the pipeline was in service.

This leads to the second cause, the fact that the fault was not detected. The reasons for this lie in PG&E's integrity management system which was simply not fit for purpose. The structure of the model, the input data and the way in which the model outputs were used were all fundamentally flawed. Despite the organisational view that this work demonstrated that risk was declining, in fact risk was uncontrolled, making a pipeline failure inevitable.

The third contributing factor, the event that actually triggered the pipeline rupture, was the higher than normal operating pressure at Milpitas Terminal. A sudden and unexpected loss of pressure control at the terminal occurred as a result of some electrical work to modify the power supply system. The work should have been controlled by the work clearance system, but the documentation was inadequate and there was apparently no consideration of the potential impact on the live gas network.

The fourth factor is the exposure of line 132 to a pressure that was sufficient to cause the line to fail. When the pressure control system failed, the operators did not intervene to prevent the supply pressure from simply flowing through to the downstream pipelines. On the other hand, they had no reason to expect that this would rupture the pipeline, as the pressure was still marginally below the maximum allowable operating pressure (MAOP). The MAOP was set too high as it had been determined using "grandfathering" provisions in the legislation that exempted the line from any testing to confirm its integrity.

These four factors would not have occurred but for a range of organisational failings that are described further below.

Causes of the Marshall pipeline rupture and release

The Marshall oil leak is the largest land-based spill in United States history, yet the causes are surprisingly simple.

The first issue is that, while the line was known to have many major cracks (as identified in multiple in-line inspections), the decision was taken not to excavate it for further visual inspection and repair. This decision was based on compliance with regulations, rather than on consideration of risk. The interpretation of the regulations was the most optimistic possible.

Second, once the line had failed, operators failed to interpret the available signs that this is what had occurred. As a result, they continued to try to pump oil through the failed line and, in doing so, severely exacerbated the size of the resultant oil spill. Their actions violated procedures and reflected a widespread culture in which procedural violations were the norm. The company had made no effort to ensure compliance with its procedures. Given this lack of commitment to procedures, a series of social psychological processes enabled the operators to dismiss warning signs and continue pumping.

Despite these apparently simple causes, preventing such an incident from recurring requires a deep understanding of why Enbridge operated in this way.

Key organisational lessons

The key organisational lessons that sit behind these immediate causes are similar — and similar to those seen in many other accident investigations. There are major lessons here for any organisation that is serious about reducing the chances of a major accident.

Latent failures and learning from small incidents

The faulty weld that led to the catastrophic events in San Bruno was made more than five decades before the pipeline ruptured. PG&E had warnings, particularly the problems in 1988, which could have given a clue that more investigation on the state of old pipelines was warranted, but these messages were not heeded. Leaks were repaired and then forgotten. The faulty weld remained a ticking time bomb just waiting to be triggered.

Latent defects like this in any system are hard to find, so any evidence of problems should be valued. Most organisations have a system in place whereby everyone is encouraged to report hazards and incidents. While such systems (usually administered by the safety department) provide a vehicle to ensure that small matters are dealt with and fixed/repaired in a timely manner, the best systems provide much broader benefits. Rather than simply being a database for action tracking, the individual incidents can be shared as stories to keep key safety messages alive. This fosters everyone's "safety imagination"[1] and helps people to link their day-to-day work with the potential for disaster.

Of course, analysis of the organisational causes sitting behind individual incidents can provide important information about key organisational vulnerabilities that are also likely to be contributing to the potential for major disaster.

Compliance

Regulatory compliance

Enbridge had direct evidence that line 6B was likely to fail (in the form of multiple sets of inspection results indicating serious cracking) and yet the evidence was not acted on. Instead, the company used strict compliance with regulatory requirements to justify delays to expensive investigation and repair work. PG&E also adopted a strict compliance approach in determining the MAOP for line 132. In these cases, compliance was not enough to avoid disaster. Compliance with standards and regulations is important but, in itself, it is not enough to prevent accidents. A "compliance is enough" mentality is a step on the road to a serious accident.

Procedural compliance

On the other hand, both accidents highlight the importance of procedural compliance. PG&E's failure to comply with its own work clearance processes and the failure of Enbridge operators to comply with shutdown requirements contributed to their respective accidents. The procedures themselves were inadequate, but greater company efforts to ensure compliance would have revealed these inadequacies and led to procedural improvement.

Effective risk management

As we have seen, another commonly used safety decision-making tool is risk assessment. We would not suggest for a moment that an assessment of the likelihood and impact of possible accidents is not worth considering. The problem comes when this information takes over and is seen to dictate, rather than contribute to, major safety decisions.

The first issue is that, in the US in particular, risk assessment tends to be used to prioritise spending to further reduce risk, rather than to reach a conclusion about whether any given situation is safe enough. Discussion about absolute risk is avoided and replaced by language about "continuous improvement". Continuous improvement is admirable, but only if risk is at an acceptable level to start with. This judgment cannot be avoided, and by ignoring this issue, processes based solely on continuous improvement are making the assumption that the status quo is safe without stating it.

Another lesson from San Bruno and Marshall is that we should all be wary of fantasy planning. We have seen that PG&E's risk-based integrity management system was divorced from field data and took on a life of its own, with complex qualitative algorithms, graphs of risk reduction and other artefacts that had no grounding in reality. This is a warning that systems can take on a symbolic value that is detached from the originally intended use of the system, especially when divorced from any real-world feedback. Risk management is always problematic when the model itself becomes reality. Those responsible for integrity management created a system based on expert judgment and a series of theoretical algorithms that satisfied the symbolic need to demonstrate that risk was controlled. Divorcing this work from real-world grounding allowed the fantasy of effective integrity management to be maintained in the face of all but a major pipeline rupture.

The final lesson for risk assessment from these pipeline disasters is this: don't fall into the trap of thinking that black swans are beyond our control and so no further effort in reducing risk is necessary or useful. Black swans *are* preventable, provided we seek out a diversity of views about the current state of risk controls and what more can be done. All major accident investigations identify precursors and warning signs. Often the issues that cause major failures are well known in some parts of the organisation. Despite this, they were either not communicated to senior management or at least not taken into account. Encouraging professional staff across organisations to exercise independent thought, have a high degree of technical curiosity, and communicate their views is hugely important, but often overlooked.

Awareness of responsibility for public safety

Finally, we saw at PG&E and Enbridge that people across the organisations failed to understand how their day-to-day activities could impact the safety of the general public. This is at least partly because the organisations failed to clearly distinguish between worker safety (so-called slips, trips and falls) and public safety. Any organisation that wants an excellent safety record must understand that preventing workers from being injured while undertaking normal tasks requires different strategies to preventing rare but catastrophic events. Both are important, but managing them requires different strategies. With process safety in particular, the absence of major incidents is not a sufficient indicator that all is well. These types of accidents have multiple controls in place to prevent them. The system can be heavily degraded without any observable change in outcome — until that last line of defence fails and with it comes catastrophe.

Why were these accidents not anticipated?

These accidents were not anticipated by senior management in either organisation. We have data that explains why this was the case at PG&E. In that organisation, senior management attention was focused on maximising profit, rather than on running a safe gas company. A focus on maximising return by cutting costs over a period of years had led to degeneration of PG&E's physical facilities. This extended to a lack of maintenance work and reduced levels of inspection. Resource constraints in the engineering area led to a lack of effective engineering support and analysis. As a result, the organisation was unable to retain corporate memory in the face of slowly developing problems.

Preventing long-term accidents such as these requires a senior management team whose members are vigilant in their focus on ensuring that safety-critical maintenance and inspection work remains up to date, despite the fact that, if they get this wrong, chances are that it will be those who come after them who will pay the price. One way to maintain senior management focus on long-term public safety is to link it to remuneration. Bonus payments are typically a major component of remuneration packages at senior company levels. Despite much organisational rhetoric that safety is the number one priority, in fact, bonus payments are typically linked to financial measures such as share price, return-on-investment or profit. It is hardly surprising therefore that senior executives favour financial performance over long-term safety when it comes to management decision-making.

The PG&E experience also suggests that the hybrid corporate structures brought about in a privatised utility sector need careful management to ensure that public and corporate interests are protected.

Implications for regulation

Regulation of both PG&E and Enbridge with regard to safety was weak. PG&E in particular had effectively been operating without regulatory oversight for several years. Having a strong and effective regulator benefits everyone, as it provides an additional layer of protection for the organisation, as well as safeguarding public interest. This requires regulations that go further than simply specifying the need for continuous improvement. It also requires an enforcement agency that has sufficient skilled resources to undertake effective audits and to follow up issues in a timely manner.

The need for ALARP

United States safety regulation in the pipeline sector (and most other hazardous industrial sectors) is based on a combination of detailed prescriptive rules and requirements for management systems. The structure of management system requirements is based on quality management ideas of continuous improvement.

Continuous improvement is an admirable idea but, as explained above, on its own, it is not sufficient to ensure that risk is adequately controlled. It assumes that risk is currently acceptable and always improving from that point. This is an enormous, but largely unstated, assumption. To put it another way, no situation is ever seen to be unacceptable under legislation based on continuous improvement.

In contrast to this, the United Kingdom and Australia have operated for many years under regulations that require companies to demonstrate that risk has been reduced to a level that is as low as reasonably practicable (ALARP). The fundamental principle is that more must be done to reduce risk until the cost of additional risk reduction is grossly disproportionate when compared to the benefit (in terms of reduced risk) gained. Said another way, the higher the risk, the more you must spend to lower it. This requirement is written into legislation, not just as part of risk assessment processes but as a general duty — an overarching principle that companies must meet.

This approach is not simple but it does provide regulators with significant additional power over recalcitrant companies when compared to legislation which is based on continuous improvement. First, the written case that risk is ALARP can be challenged until an appropriate justification is provided. Then audits and inspections can be targeted at checking that companies are doing what they said they would do. Any deviation from that is a clear regulatory breach.

This type of regulatory approach has been recommended in the US following the *Deepwater Horizon* disaster, but it is still under debate. Our analysis of these pipeline sector events shows that this sector would benefit from an ALARP-style regime too.

The perils of grandfathering
Many countries are now facing the challenge of how to manage ongoing operations of ageing industrial facilities that do not comply with current design standards. In an ALARP-based regulatory regime, such issues are resolved by considering risk. There is no requirement for blanket compliance, but neither is there blanket exemption. When major changes to standards occur, companies are required to identify where old facilities do not comply and to justify their proposed course of action based on consideration of both risk and cost. In this way, potentially high-risk deviations are at least investigated and minor things can be ignored.

In contrast, in the US, there is a process known as "grandfathering" whereby old facilities are often given blanket exemption from meeting new requirements. This was the case for determining the maximum allowable operating pressure for pipelines and for upgrading plant venting and flaring systems at the BP Texas City Refinery before the major fire at that site in 2005.[2]

The justification for exemption is typically made by industry lobby groups on the basis that there is no evidence that the issue in question is a problem. As described earlier, this argument must be used with great care when it comes to major accidents.

Effective implementation
PG&E's integrity management system was audited in 2005 and then not again until 2010. This was apparently typical of the CPUC's "light touch" enforcement policy. As discussed in Chapter 6, lack of experienced personnel to oversee the gas industry was a major limitation for the CPUC.

This is also highlighted in the CPUC audits themselves. The San Bruno experience raises questions about the nature, scope and effectiveness of regulatory audits. While the CPUC 2005 audit found some significant limitations in PG&E's integrity management system, these issues were never followed up by the regulator. This raises the issue of graduated enforcement tools and the need for a range of strategies on the part of regulators to promote industry action. Such tools can range from safety promotion and encouragement through to prosecution.

Finally, the San Bruno incident highlights potential problems when utility entities are subject to economic regulation controlling cost to consumers, and also to technical regulation aimed at protecting the public from physical harm. The gas industry in many countries has a broadly similar industry structure and the safety implications of this could be the subject of further research.

Take-away messages

All organisations are potentially at risk of experiencing the same problems seen at PG&E and Enbridge. To assist in thinking about which issues might be most relevant to your organisation, we invite you to consider the following set of targeted questions which are aimed at highlighting key issues for consideration. Of importance in each case is the answer to the question, but also how confident you are of that answer. Are your responses based on evidence, or simply your assumption of what you believe to be the case?

- How effective is our work clearance system in anticipating and managing the operational impact of planned maintenance etc?
- If a major accident were to occur, would our control room personnel recognise the need to shut down immediately? Would they feel empowered to take the necessary action?
- For old facilities, what is our approach to compliance with current standards? To what extent do we "grandfather" without assessing risk? Who makes these decisions?
- When people in our organisation review documents, do they understand what they are taking responsibility for and what action they should take if they are unsatisfied?
- In what ways does our integrity management system resemble the one in place at PG&E before the rupture? Are the data in our integrity management databases, and the decisions made based on that data, grounded in reality? How do we know we are doing enough inspections, and the right inspections, using the right methods?

- Are the resources allocated to our activities to maintain facility integrity driven by risk or cost? How do we know we are spending enough?
- How do we decide when known safety problems require repair? How do such decisions balance risk and cost? How confident are we that known minor problems are not about to become serious accidents?
- Do all of our employees (field and office staff) understand the links between their actions and public safety outcomes?
- Does our organisation understand the difference between public (process) safety and workplace safety, right to the top management level?
- Are we too focused on regulatory compliance for its own sake? Have we lost sight of the reason why actions linked to safety are taken?
- To what extent is expert technical knowledge and a questioning attitude valued in our professional staff?
- Can we be sure that our operators are complying with safety critical procedures?
- Can we really claim that we know that risk from our facilities is ALARP, or are we waiting for evidence of problems before we look hard at the effectiveness of our risk controls? How hard do we look for warning signs?
- To what extent do we see the absence of problems as reassurance about system integrity? What are our key exposures to the potential for latent errors?
- Is information about leaks and data on inspection findings reviewed for trends, rather than just followed up for repair? How are stories of past defects and leaks (ours and others) kept alive in our organisation?
- Are we rewarding senior management for the right behaviours? What messages do our senior managers give to the rest of the organisation on public safety?
- To what extent do we value detailed technical industry experience in senior management? Is membership of our senior management committees balanced between technical expertise and governance functions, such as finance and legal?
- Are we up to date with internal audits? Do we follow up findings in a timely manner? Are people held accountable?

Endnotes

1   Pidgeon, N and O'Leary, M, "Man-made disasters: why technology and organizations (sometimes) fail", *Safety Science* 2000, 34: 15–30.

2   Hopkins, A, *Failure to learn: the BP Texas City Refinery disaster*, CCH Australia Limited, Sydney, 2008.

Chapter

11

APPENDIX

COMBINING RISK SCORES FOR INDIVIDUAL THREATS

As described in Chapter 5, PG&E (and Enbridge) used risk index modelling to determine an overall risk score for each segment in their pipeline network and so prioritise inspection activities. In this Appendix, we describe how the overall score was derived from the individual factor scores and the problems with the approach adopted.

PG&E's intention was to combine risk scores from different threats into one overall measure of the probability of failure of the pipeline. The method was based on the following equation:

$$LOF = 0.25EC + 0.45TP + 0.20GM + 0.10DM^1$$

where:

- LOF is likelihood of failure
- EC is likelihood of failure due to external corrosion
- TP is likelihood of failure due to third-party interference
- GM is likelihood of failure due to ground movement
- DM is likelihood of failure due to design and materials.

The weightings applied to the probability of each threat are described by PG&E as being the proportion of pipeline leaks due to each of these causes. The NTSB has criticised the prioritisation system because, as shown in Table A.1, the historical proportion of leaks is not as the PG&E procedure indicates.[2]

TABLE A.1: Weightings of individual threats versus leak history

Threat	Weighting in PG&E procedure	Actual proportion of leaks 2004 to 2010
External corrosion	0.25	0.51
Third-party interference	0.45	0.24
Ground movement	0.20	0
Design and materials	0.10	0.24

In fact, the problem with this approach is more fundamental. The historical data represents an *average* of leaks throughout the PG&E network. It does not provide a deterministic indication of the reasons why any *individual* pipeline segment might fail. In an operating system, that determination must be made for each segment independently. Another way of explaining the flawed logic of the PG&E system is to note that a segment with a serious materials problem is likely to leak. That potential is not reduced because the same line may not be particularly vulnerable to external corrosion or third-party interference, but that is the effect of averaging scores across threats.

This can be thought of as a problem of representativeness. For one pipeline segment chosen at random from the network, if we have no other information about the segment, we can only assume that its vulnerability to leaks is that of the average for the system as a whole. But that segment is one of thousands in the system, and we know that the vulnerability of segments to threats covers a wide range. As soon as we have more information about any particular segment (in the form of index scores for each threat), our best estimate of the vulnerability of the segment is no longer represented by the average. The segment is then part of a smaller group that has particular vulnerabilities due to age, location etc.

In fact, if the individual scores represent the probability of failure due to each threat, then the correct way to combine them is to consider the probability of *survival* in the face of all four identified threats. If each index is a score out of 100, where a higher score represents a higher vulnerability to that threat, then the risk index represents a probability of failure (over an unspecified time). The probability of survival is then 1 minus the probability of failure. The overall probability of failure for the segment from all threats is then:

Estimated probability of failure = 1 − Estimated probability of survival

Estimated probability of survival =
$(1 - EC/100) \times (1 - TP/100) \times (1 - GM/100) \times (1 - DM/100)$

where EC, TP etc are the scores for each identified threat.

The probabilities are multiplied in this case because integrity of the segment requires survival from all of the threats, ie external corrosion AND third-party interference AND ground movement etc.

Two segments with identical risk index scores (based on adding scores of individual threats) can have very different failure probabilities, especially if one particularly bad score is masked by good scores on other indices. This is illustrated in Table A.2 where the segment represented by scenario 2 has a much greater chance of failure than scenario 1. Despite identical risk index scores, scenario 2 scores very badly on corrosion and so is much more likely to fail.

TABLE A.2: Calculating a "failure probability score" from an index sum[3]

	Scenario 1		Scenario 2	
	Index score	Probability of failure score (%)	Index score	Probability of failure score (%)
External corrosion	40		90	
Third-party interference	30		10	
Ground movement	20		10	
Design and materials	30		10	
Total	120	76.48	120	92.71

It must be noted that equating risk index scores generated by qualitative methods to failure frequencies is a major assumption, but these scores are designed to give a relative indication. What we are attempting to show here is that, even putting aside questions about how the individual scores were generated, the way in which they were combined to give one overall risk index is mathematically incorrect and as a consequence the results can be seriously misleading.

PG&E was aware that the ranking system it had adopted was problematic, as shown by the way in which it chose to treat internal corrosion as a threat. It noted that only 2% of its network is subject to internal corrosion, and so it has not been included in the ranking by the averaging system described in Table A.1 because, "rather than dilute the risk calculation for the remaining 98% of the pipeline system, pipelines with these threats were prioritized as 'high risk' and the likelihood factors were not included in the overall risk calculation".[4] Of course, the same argument applies to every other threat. If the risk of leakage due to one threat is high, it is not diminished just because other threats may not be present.

While the discussion here has focused on the PG&E system, it must be said that the Enbridge system suffers from the same fundamental problem. Looking at the Enbridge system at the time of the Marshall incident, its risk index model had been expanded to include six (or in some cases, seven) factors. Enbridge includes categories for dents and cracks (in addition to mechanisms that cause dents and cracks), presumably in an attempt to factor in known faults and flaws and the potential for these to escalate to failure of a segment. It summed the individual risk indices to determine an overall score for each segment, although documentation indicates major changes over the years as to what weighting factors should be applied to the individual scores. It is almost as if those in charge of the model knew that there was an inconsistency here but did not know what to do about it.

Endnotes

1   PG&E, *Procedure for risk management RMP-01* (downloaded from the CPUC website), p 8. Available at www.cpuc.ca.gov/PUC/sanbrunoreport.htm.

2   NTSB, *Pacific Gas and Electric Company natural gas transmission pipeline rupture and fire, San Bruno, CA, September 9, 2010*, pipeline accident report, Washington DC, 2011, section 2.6.2.1. Available at www.ntsb.gov/doclib/reports/2011/par1101.pdf.

3   Based on Muhlbauer, WK, *Pipeline risk management manual: ideas, techniques and resources*, Gulf Professional Publishing, Burlington, Massachusetts, 2004, Table 14.12, p 14/300, although in Muhlbauer's scheme, high-risk index scores are good, whereas in the PG&E system high scores are bad.

4   PG&E, *Procedure for risk management RMP-01* (downloaded from the CPUC website), p 4. Available at www.cpuc.ca.gov/PUC/sanbrunoreport.htm.

BIBLIOGRAPHY

Achenbach, J, *A hole at the bottom of the sea: the race to kill the BP Oil gusher*, Simon and Schuster, New York, 2011.

American Petroleum Institute, *API recommended practice 754: Process safety performance indicators for the refining and petrochemical undustries*, 2010.

American Society of Mechanical Engineers, *B31.8S Managing system integrity of gas pipelines*, 2012.

Avery, S, *The pipeline and the paradigm: Keystone XL, tar sands and the battle to diffuse the carbon bomb*, Ruka Press, Washington DC, 2013.

Ayres, I and Braithwaite, J, *Responsive regulation: transcending the deregulation debate*, Oxford University Press, New York, 1992.

Baker, J, et al, *The report of the BP US refineries independent safety review panel*, BP, London, 2007.

Bergin, T, *Spills and spin: the inside story of BP*, Random House, London, 2011.

Bluff, L and Gunningham, N, "Principle, process, performance or what? New approaches to OHS standards setting", in Bluff, L, Gunningham, N and Johnstone, R (eds), *OHS regulation for a changing world of work*, The Federation Press, Sydney, 2004.

Bluff, L and Johnstone, R, *The relationship between "reasonably practicable" and risk management regulation*, working paper 27, National Research Centre for OHS Regulation, Canberra, 2004. Available at http://regnet.anu.edu.au/publications/wp-27-relationship-between-reasonably-practicable-and-risk-management-regulation.

Bourrier, M, "Elements for designing a self-correcting organization: examples from nuclear power plants", in Hale, AR and Baram, M (eds), *Safety management: the challenge of change*, Pergamon, Oxford, 1998.

Bourrier, M, "The legacy of the high reliability organization project", *Journal of Contingencies and Crisis Management*, 2011, 19: 9–13.

CAIB [Columbia Accident Investigation Board], report, vol 1, National Aeronautics and Space Administration, 2003.

Clarke, L, *Mission improbable: using fantasy documents to tame disaster*, University of Chicago Press, Chicago, 1999.

CPUC, *Report of the independent review panel, San Bruno explosion*, prepared for the CPUC, revised copy, 24 June 2011. Available at www.cpuc.ca.gov/NR/rdonlyres/85E17CDA-7CE2-4D2D-93BA-B95D25CF98B2/0/cpucfinalreportrevised62411.pdf.

CPUC, *Incident investigation report, September 9, 2010 PG&E pipeline rupture in San Bruno, California* (released 12 January 2012), CPUC, Consumer Protection & Safety Division, San Francisco, 2012. Available at www.cpuc.ca.gov/NR/rdonlyres/28720A78-1DC7-4474-B51F-00C5E8BB5069/0/AgendaStaffReportreOIIPGESanBrunoExplosion.pdf.

Cullen, WD, *The public inquiry into the Piper Alpha disaster*, HMSO, London, 1990.

Dekker, S, *Just culture: balancing safety and accountability*, Ashgate, Aldershot, 2007.

Deming, WE, *Out of the crisis*, MIT Press, Cambridge, 2000.

Donley, P, *This is not about mystics: or why a little science would help a lot*, Deepwater Horizon study group working paper, 2011, pp 11, 18.

Doorn, N and Van de Poel, I, "Editors' overview: moral responsibility in technology and engineering", *Science and Engineering Ethics* 2012, 18: 1–11.

Enbridge Inc, *2009 annual report: where energy meets people*, 2009.

Farley, M, "California proposes major changes to refinery process safety management (PSM) standard", *The National Law Review*, 19 September 2014. Available at www.natlawreview.com/article/california-proposes-major-changes-to-refinery-process-safety-management-psm-standard.

Flin, R, O'Connor, P and Crichton, M, *Safety at the sharp end: a guide to non-technical skills*, Ashgate, Aldershot, 2008.

Gawande, A, *The checklist manifesto*, Macmillan, 2010.

Hale, A and Borys, D, "Working to rule, or working safely? Part 1: a state of the art review", *Safety Science* 2013, 55: 207–221.

Hale, A and Borys, D, "Working to rule, or working safely? Part 2: the management of safety rules and procedures", *Safety Science* 2013, 55: 222–231.

Hale, A, Borys, D and Adams, M, "Safety regulation: the lessons of workplace safety rule management for managing the regulatory burden", *Safety Science*, DOI: 10.1016/j.ssci.2013.11.012 (in press).

Hale, A, Goossens, L and Van de Poel, I, "Oil and gas industry regulation: from detailed technical inspection to assessment of safety management", in Kirwan, B, Hale, A and Hopkins, A (eds), *Changing regulation: controlling risks in society*, Pergamon, Oxford, 2002.

Hale, AR, Heijer, T and Koornneef, F, "Management of safety rules: the case of the railways", *Safety Science Monitor* 2003, 7(1): 1–11.

Hale, AR and Swuste, P, "Safety rules: procedural freedom or action constraint?", *Safety Science* 1998, 29: 163–177.

Haukelid, K, "Theories of (safety) culture revisited — an anthropological approach", *Safety Science* 2008, 46: 413–426.

Hayes, J, "Incident reporting: a nuclear industry case study", in Hopkins, A (ed), *Learning from high reliability organisations*, CCH Australia Limited, Sydney, 2009.

Hayes, J, "Operator competence and capacity — lessons from the Montara blowout", *Safety Science* 2012, 50: 563–574.

Hayes, J, "A new direction in offshore safety regulation", in Baram, M, Lindoe, P and Renn, O (eds), *Governing risk in offshore oil and gas operations*, Cambridge University Press, Cambridge, 2013.

Hayes, J, *Operational decision-making in high-hazard organizations: drawing a line in the sand*, Ashgate, Farnham, 2013.

Hayes, J, "The role of professionals in managing technological hazards: the Montara blowout", in Lockie, S, Sonnenfeld, DA and Fisher, DR (eds), *Routledge international handbook of social and environmental change*, Routledge, London, 2013.

Hayes, J and Hopkins, A, "Deepwater Horizon — lessons for the pipeline industry", *Journal of Pipeline Engineering* 2012, 11(3): 145–153.

Hayes, J and Maslen, S, "Knowing stories that matter: learning for effective safety decision-making", *Journal of Risk Research*, 2014, DOI: 10.1080/13669877. 2014.910690.

Hopkins, A, "A culture of denial: sociological similarities between the Moura and Gretley mine disasters", *Journal of Occupational Health and Safety — Australia and New Zealand* 2000, 16(1): 29–36.

Hopkins, A, "Was Three Mile Island a 'normal Accident'?", *Journal of Contingencies and Crisis Management* 2001, 9(2): 65–72.

Hopkins, A, "Two models of major hazard regulation: recent Australian experience", in Kirwan, B, Hale, A and Hopkins, A (eds), *Changing regulation: controlling risks in society*, Pergamon, Oxford, 2002.

Hopkins, A, "Beyond compliance monitoring: new strategies for safety regulators", *Law and Policy* 2007, 29(2): 210–225.

Hopkins, A, *Failure to learn: the BP Texas City Refinery disaster*, CCH Australia Limited, Sydney, 2008.

Hopkins, A, "Identifying and responding to warnings", in Hopkins, A (ed), *Learning from high reliability organisations*, CCH Australia Limited, Sydney, 2009.

Hopkins, A, "Risk-management and rule-compliance: decision-making in hazardous industries", *Safety Science* 2011, 49: 110–120.

Hopkins, A, *Disastrous decisions: the human and organisational causes of the Gulf of Mexico blowout*, CCH Australia Limited, Sydney, 2012.

Hopkins, A, *Explaining safety case*, working paper 87, National Research Centre for OHS Regulation, Canberra, 2013. Available at http://regnet.anu.edu.au/publications/wp-87-explaining-%E2%80%9Csafety-case%E2%80%9D.

Hopkins, A, *The cost benefit hurdle for safety case regulation*, working paper 88, National Research Centre for OHS Regulation, Canberra, 2014. Available at http://regnet.anu.edu.au/publications/wp-88-cost-benefit-hurdle-safety-case-regulation.

Hopkins, A, and Maslen, S, *Risky rewards: how company bonuses affect safety*, Ashgate, Aldershot, 2015.

HSE [UK Health and Safety Executive], *An interim evaluation of the Offshore Installation (Safety Case) Regulations 1992*, HSE, Norwich, 1995.

HSE, *Literature review on the perceived benefits and disadvantages of UK safety case regimes*, HSE, Norwich, 2003.

Hudson, P and van der Graaf, GC, *The rule of three: situation awareness in hazardous situations*, SPE 46765, Society of Petroleum Engineers International Conference on Health, Safety, and Environment in Oil and Gas Exploration and Production, Caracas, Venezuela, 7 to 10 June 1998.

Janis, I, *Groupthink: psychological studies of policy decisions and fiascos*, Houghton Mifflin, Boston, 1982.

Karau, SJ and Williams, KD, "Social loafing: a meta-analytic review and theoretical integration", *Journal of Personality and Social Psychology* 1993, 65: 681–706.

Kirwan, B, Hale, A and Hopkins, A, "Insights into safety regulation", in Kirwan, B, Hale, A and Hopkins, A (eds), *Changing regulation: controlling risks in society*, Pergamon, Oxford, 2002.

Klein, GA, *Streetlights and shadows: searching for the keys to adaptive decision making*, MIT Press, Cambridge, Massachusetts, 2009.

Leveson, N, *The use of safety cases in certification and regulation*, MIT ESD technical report, 2011. Available at http://sunnyday.mit.edu/safer-world.

Maslen, S, "Organisational factors for learning in the Australian gas pipeline industry", *Journal of Risk Research* 2014, DOI: 10.1080/13669877.2014.919514.

Maslen, S and Hayes, J, "Experts under the microscope: the Wivenhoe Dam case", *Environment Systems and Decisions* 2014, 34(2): 183–193.

Maurino, D, Reason, J, Johnston, N and Lee, R, *Beyond aviation human factors*, Ashgate, Aldershot, 1995.

McIntyre, GR, *Patterns in safety thinking: a literature guide to air transportation safety*, Ashgate, Aldershot, 2000.

Middlehurst, R and Kennie, T, "Leading professionals: towards new concepts of professionalism", in Broadbent, J, Dietrich, M and Roberts, J (eds), *The end of the professions? The restructuring of professional work*, Routledge, London, 1997.

Muhlbauer, WK, *Pipeline risk management manual: ideas, techniques and resources*, Gulf Professional Publishing, Burlington, Massachusetts, 2004.

National Commission on the BP Deepwater Horizon Oil Spill and Offshore Drilling, *Deepwater: the Gulf oil disaster and the future of offshore drilling, report to the President*, 2011.

National Commission on the BP Deepwater Horizon Oil Spill and Offshore Drilling, *Macondo: the Gulf oil disaster, Chief Counsel's report*, Washington, 2011.

Nickerson, R, "Confirmation bias: a ubiquitous phenomenon in many guises", *Review of General Psychology* 1998, 2: 175–220.

NTSB, *Texas Eastern Gas Pipeline Company ruptures and fires at Beaumont, Kentucky, on April 27, 1985, and Lancaster, Kentucky, on February 21, 1986*, pipeline accident report NTSB/PAR-87/01, Washington DC, 1987.

NTSB, *Pacific Gas and Electric Company natural gas transmission pipeline rupture and fire, San Bruno, CA, September 9, 2010*, pipeline accident report, Washington DC, 2011. Available at www.ntsb.gov/doclib/reports/2011/par1101.pdf.

NTSB, *Enbridge Incorporated hazardous liquid pipeline rupture and release, Marshall, Michigan, July 25, 2010*, pipeline accident report, Washington DC, 2012.

Ocasio, W, "The opacity of risk: language and the culture of safety in NASA's space shuttle program", in Starbuck, WH and Farjoun, M (eds), *Organization at the limit: lessons from the Columbia disaster*, Blackwell, Malden, Massachusetts, 2005.

OGP [International Association of Oil and Gas Producers], *Cognitive issues associated with process safety and environmental incidents*, report no. 460, 2012.

Oh, JIH, "The EU Seveso II Directive: an example of a regulation that could act as an initiator to raise the major hazard safety awareness within society", in Kirwan, B, Hale, A and Hopkins, A (eds), *Changing regulation: controlling risks in society*, Pergamon, Oxford, 2002.

OSHA [Occupational Safety & Health Administration], *1910.119 Process safety management of highly hazardous chemicals*.

Overland Consulting, *Focused audit of Pacific Gas & Electric gas transmission pipeline safety-related expenditures for the period 1996 to 2010*, Leawood, Kansas, 30 December 2011 (for CPUC).

Paté-Cornell, E, "On 'black swans' and 'perfect storms': risk analysis and management when statistics are not enough", *Risk Analysis* 2012, 32(11): 1823–1833.

Paterson, J, *Behind the mask: regulating health and safety in Britain's offshore oil and gas industry*, Ashgate, Aldershot, 2000.

Pidgeon, N and O'Leary, M, "Man-made disasters: why technology and organizations (sometimes) fail", *Safety Science* 2000, 34: 15–30.

Polanyi, M, *The tacit dimension*, Doubleday, New York, 1967.

Pronovost, P, *Safe patients, smart hospitals: how one doctor's checklist can help us change health care from the inside out*, Hudson, New York, 2010.

Reason, J, *Managing the risks of organizational accidents*, Ashgate, Aldershot, 1997.

Reason, J, *The human contribution: unsafe acts, accidents and heroic recoveries*, Ashgate, Farnham, 2008.

Rose, D and Crescent, J, *Evaluation of the offshore safety legislative regime in the UK*, Society of Petroleum Engineers International Conference on Health, Safety, and the Environment in Oil and Gas Exploration and Production, Stavanger, Norway, 26 to 28 June 2000.

Salmon, PM, Stanton, NA and Young, KL, "Situation awareness on the road: review, theoretical and methodological issues, and future directions", *Theoretical Issues in Ergonomics Science* 2012, 13: 472–492.

Schein, E, *Organisational culture and leadership*, Jossey-Bass, San Francisco, 1992.

Schobel, M, "Compliance with safety rules: the role of environmental structures", in Itoigawa, N, Wilpert, B and Fahlbruch, B (eds), *Emerging demands for the safety of nuclear power operations*, CRC Press, Boca Raton, 2005.

Smith, R and Woo, S, "Calls for action emerge after gas explosion", *Wall Street Journal*, 14 September 2010.

Sneddon, A, Mearns, K and Flin, R, "Stress, fatigue, situation awareness and safety in offshore drilling crews", *Safety Science* 2013, 56: 80–88.

Snook, SA, *Friendly fire: the accidental shootdown of US Black Hawks over Northern Iraq*, Princeton University Press, Princeton, New Jersey, 2000.

Song, L and McGowan, E, "The dilbit disaster: inside the biggest oil spill you've never heard of", *Inside Climate News*, 2012.

Taleb, NN, *The black swan*, Penguin, London, 2010.

Turner, BA and Pidgeon, NF, *Man-made disasters*, Butterworths, Oxford, 1997.

US Chemical Safety and Hazard Investigation Board, *Regulatory report: Chevron Richmond Refinery pipe rupture and fire*, report no. 2012-03-I-CA, May 2014.

Vaughan, D, *The Challenger launch decision: risky technology, culture and deviance at NASA*, University of Chicago Press, Chicago, 1996.

VECTRA, *Literature review of the perceived benefits and disadvantages of the UK safety case regimes*, HSE, London, 2003.

Vinnem, JE, "Analysis of root causes of major hazard precursors in the Norwegian offshore petroleum industry", *Reliability Engineering and System Safety*, 2010 (accepted manuscript).

Weaver, J, "Offshore safety in the wake of the Macondo disaster: business as usual or a sea change?", *Houston Journal of International Law* Winter 2014: 147–216.

Weick, KE and Sutcliffe, KM, *Managing the unexpected: assuring high performance in an age of complexity*, Jossey-Bass, San Francisco, 2001.

Weick, KE, Sutcliffe, KM and Obstfeld, D, "Organizing for high reliability: processes of collective mindfulness", in Sutton, RI and Staw, BM (eds), *Research in organizational behavior*, JAI Press Inc, Stamford, 1999.

Williams, J, "New frontiers for regulatory interaction within the UK nuclear industry", in Kirwan, B, Hale, A and Hopkins, A (eds), *Changing regulation: controlling risks in society*, Pergamon, Oxford, 2002.

INDEX

CPSIA information can be obtained at www.ICGtesting.com
Printed in the USA
LVOW11s1127060216

473996LV00013B/375/P